P9-ARW-727

NEW DIRECTIONS
FOR EXPERIENTIAL
LEARNING

Number 12 • 1981

NEW DIRECTIONS FOR EXPERIENTIAL LEARNING

A Quarterly Sourcebook
Pamela J. Tate, Editor-in-Chief
Morris T. Keeton, Consulting Editor
Sponsored by the Council for the Advancement of Experiential Learning (CAEL)

Number 12, 1981

Clarifying Learning Outcomes in the Liberal Arts

Georgine Loacker
Ernest G. Palola
Editors

Jossey-Bass Inc., Publishers
San Francisco • Washington • London

CLARIFYING LEARNING OUTCOMES IN THE LIBERAL ARTS
New Directions for Experiential Learning
Number 12, 1981
Georgine Loacker, Ernest G. Palola, Editors

New Directions for Experiential Learning is published quarterly by Jossey-Bass Inc., Publishers. Subscriptions are available at the regular rate for institutions, libraries, and agencies of $30 for one year. Individuals may subscribe at the special professional rate of $18 for one year.

Correspondence:
Subscriptions, single-issue orders, change of address notices, undelivered copies, and other correspondence should be sent to *New Directions* Subscriptions, Jossey-Bass Inc., Publishers, 433 California Street, San Francisco, California 94104.

Editorial correspondence should be sent to the Editor-in-Chief, Pamela J. Tate or the Consulting Editor, Morris T. Keeton at the Council for the Advancement of Experiential Learning (CAEL), Suite 300, Lakefront North, Columbia, Maryland 21044.

Library of Congress Catalogue Card Number LC 80-84276

International Standard Serial Number ISSN 0271-0595

International Standard Book Number ISBN 87589-827-0

Cover design by Willi Baum

Manufactured in the United States of America

Contents

Editors' Notes

Why a discussion of clarifying learning outcomes in a series on experiential learning? Both are innovative approaches to education that have gained greatly in currency in recent years, though each can also claim a venerable lineage in educational thought and practice. Both can be seen as responsive to the particular needs and interests of the new majority in higher education—the adult learner who has become accustomed to learning by doing outside the academy and often has rather definite ideas about what returning to the academic setting should yield in return for the time, effort, and money he or she expends.

But the most important similarities between the two approaches have to do with learning: Research verifies our intuitive sense that learning which includes both an active participatory dimension and a cognitive intake of information is more rapid, more effective, and more durable—the same results that are verified for learning in which the intended goals or outcomes are made clear beforehand (see the Coleman chapter in Keeton, 1976; Kozma, Belle, and Williams, 1978, Chapters Sixteen and Seventeen; Lenning, 1977). Clarifying learning outcomes and experiential learning are among the most powerful influences we have been able to identify for enhancing the quality of learning. And it is no surprise that they intersect. Educators who have explored either approach can testify (as many in this sourcebook do) that you cannot engage in either for long without beginning to think seriously about the other.

We recognize that traditionally most faculty have been concerned about what their students should and do learn, and have designed learning experiences to achieve that, but in this sourcebook we draw a distinction between this familiar traditional approach and one that begins by specifying outcomes at the outset of the learning process. A few words about these two approaches will shed light on this distinction.

In most of what we understand as the teaching process in higher education, tradition defines what students should learn and why it is important. Seldom do faculty question the legitimacy of standard components of disciplinary content. Often they select what to teach on the basis of the opinions of outside authorities such as text authors, themes within the discipline, or an interpretation carried from graduate study. They define the amount of content by how much will fit within a term, and compute

We wish to express our gratitude to Joan Muller at Empire State College and Isabelle Cox and Diana Piotrowski of Alverno College for hours spent typing manuscripts. We would also like to thank Dr. Mark Hein, director of higher education publications at Alverno College, for his excellent assistance in editing the final draft of several chapters in this volume.

credit value from the term length and contact time expected between faculty and students in class groups.

Perspectives in this book will point to a process that builds on and extends the traditional approach. Faculty concern for what students learn becomes a definite commitment to making learning results—both cognitive and affective—explicit and to evaluating that learning with appropriate instruments. Assessment is an important component of a learning outcomes approach, because the learning may have been the result of a carefully organized instructional activity such as a course or of an experience that may not have been designed primarily for learning at all, as when a returning adult reflects on learning from life and work experiences. In either case, faculty are responsible for designing or eliciting and approving the design of a course of study to achieve a specific purpose, thus giving attention to why certain activities are included and what learning results from their accomplishments. They integrate each part deliberately into a total picture, much as an artist manipulates a medium through intended strokes to produce the completed product. Learning outcomes developed by so deliberate a process are "ends by design" and, stated explicitly in learning contracts and courses, are in fact "ends by design through specified means."

This sourcebook assumes that thinking about and implementing the process of clarifying intended learning outcomes is itself a worthwhile learning experience, both personally and professionally, because it leads faculty to rethink the consequences of their approaches to teaching and makes the learning process negotiable for the learner. Admittedly, not all postsecondary educators are of one mind on the merits of goal-oriented learning. Some critics have suggested that it may be only a fad, stimulated by institutional concerns for economic survival and consumer pressures for accountability on the part of higher education (Goldsmith and Pottinger, 1979). Though we accept the possibility that economic pressures may be acting as important catalysts to prompt changes long overdue in higher education, there is evidence that the process of clarifying learning outcomes has been much more than a short-term market strategy on the part of institutions; it has proven to be a lively stimulant to the improvement of teaching and to the renewal of entire institutions. Therefore, through highlighting strategies for clarifying learning outcomes in various fields, we hope to encourage educators to consider goal-oriented approaches to learning as one way to strengthen the faculty role, challenge students to be more self-directed, and contribute to both the survival and quality of higher education.

It should be mentioned that the strategies presented here were developed and implemented primarily by faculty. In some institutions, students have taken key roles in the definition, clarification, and use of outcomes. But whether students participate in defining outcomes (as in many prior and contract learning programs) or whether faculty define outcomes from their own experience as educators (as in several liberal arts and professional programs), the student's activity and performance is always the empirical source for determining which outcomes have actually occurred and which should next be sought.

The matters at hand in this sourcebook are also of importance to administrators as those charged to acquire, shape, and deliver institutional support to the teaching/learning interaction. Clarifying learning outcomes can help to clarify institutional priorities as to which instructional resources are most critically needed and in what forms; the process also has a tremendous effect upon student records, facility and staff planning, faculty evaluation and development, and every other support service rendered to faculty and students. Administrators who are seeking renewal of their institution and clarification of its mission may find outcomes clarification a congenial strategy well worth the cost.

This sourcebook is organized into seven chapters, providing readers with information derived from serious efforts to clarify educational outcomes in different ways. The chapter by Mauksch focuses on the need for a supportive environment that will enable faculty to take a serious look at clarifying outcomes and its implications for their teaching. The author sets forth the systematic efforts of one national professional organization to create such an environment for the members of its discipline. The chapter by Bradley and Bolman reinforces the need for such an environment by raising questions about the current responsibilities of faculty and enumerating forces in the contemporary world that call for articulated learning goals and at the same time threaten the professional nature of the faculty role. The chapter challenges faculty to turn that threat to their advantage by taking hold of curriculum design from several vantage points.

The chapter by Loacker probes the clarifying of outcomes in individual disciplines in relation to liberal arts degree programs. In examining what the faculty in eleven different institutions have done, the chapter analyzes how clarifying outcomes has begun, proceeded, and affected the life of students, faculty, and the entire institution.

The chapters by Harrisberger and by Greenblatt and Striby focus on specific needs regarding the clarifying of outcomes in two different fields. Harrisberger's chapter suggests how engineering educators are beginning to identify the need to specify learning outcomes and to design related teaching activities—despite the formidable internal resistance that seems directly proportionate to the material success of graduate engineers. The chapter deals with outcomes traditionally associated with the liberal arts and the significance of these outcomes for engineers. Greenblatt and Striby's chapter details the need for art educators to clarify expected outcomes so that faculty can design sequential curricula and learners can demonstrate abilities developed in the process of creating art but not always observable in the product.

The chapter by Palola and Evans considers learning outcomes from an entirely different perspective—that of the learner. It examines data on the interaction between student and faculty in several individualized programs—with focus on a specific institution as a case study. It draws observations and raises questions about the impact of faculty role on the articulating and achieving of outcomes in the context of the student learning process.

The chapter by Evans, Loacker, and Palola summarizes the volume, identifying what we have learned from the authors about ways to approach clarifying outcomes. This chapter highlights the process of identifying outcomes by setting forth components for faculty and administrators to organize into a model unique for their institution. Finally, it suggests some future directions we think it important to consider.

Renewal—of the learning process, of the people who engage in it, and of the institutions where learning occurs—is ultimately the goal of this book. Of course we realize that renewal is not a one-time effort; it requires a regular and continuous process, one that at each stage enlivens and reenergizes organizational life (Palola and Padgett, 1971; Bergquist and Shoemaker, 1976). Renewal also requires sustained consensus and commitment and a variety of strategies affecting every area of institutional life, from mission statements to facilities usage, from learning outcomes to budget allocations. Nonetheless, we have seen from several faculties' experience that defining learning outcomes is a singularly potent strategy. It can be a rare opportunity to rethink the educational purposes for which an institution exists and to state them so clearly that they can once again be used to shape the institution's acquisition and allocation of its human and physical resources. We have also seen how such a process can increase the institution's given resources by augmenting the level of consensus and commitment among its members—the productive energy that makes an institution work.

The opportunity for such renewal could hardly come at a better time. The mission of higher education and the market it serves are no longer unified or even coherent: Diverse populations of new students, making demands that were once ignored as coming from the world outside the walls, now constitute a majority of those who seek undergraduate and graduate education. In the last century, taking the meaning and value of education for granted, we have come perilously close to dotting the nation's landscape with replicas of two or three dominant models. Now, if we can clarify the distinctive outcomes we seek, we may rediscover that vital diversity that should characterize a free society and upon which its survival and that of our respective institutions depends.

Georgine Loacker
Ernest G. Palola
Editors

References

Bergquist, W., and Shoemaker, W. (Eds.). *New Directions for Higher Education: A Comprehensive Approach to Institutional Development,* no. 15. San Francisco: Jossey-Bass, 1976.

Goldsmith, J., and Pottinger, P. S. "Future Directions." In P. S. Pottinger and J. Goldsmith (Eds.). *New Directions for Experiential Learning: Defining Measuring Competence,* no. 3. San Francisco: Jossey-Bass, 1979.

Keeton, M. *Experiential Learning: Rationale, Characteristics, and Assessment.* San Francisco: Jossey-Bass, 1976.

Kozma, R. B., Belle, L. W., and Williams, G. W. *Instructional Techniques in Higher Education.* Englewood Cliffs, N.J.: Educational Technology Publications, 1978.

Lenning, O. *A Structure for the Outcomes of Postsecondary Education.* Boulder, Colo.: National Center for Higher Education Management Systems, 1977.

Palola, E., and Padgett, W. *Planning for Self-Renewal.* Berkeley: Center for Research and Development in Higher Education, University of California, 1971.

Georgine Loacker is chair of the Division of Communications and of the Assessment Council at Alverno College, Milwaukee, Wisconsin. As a professor of English at Alverno, she participated in the development of its outcome-oriented education and has served as consultant to liberal arts faculty in colleges and universities that have sought to identify and/or assess learning outcomes. She has served as a board member and regional manager for the Council for the Advancement of Experiential Learning (CAEL), as welll as designer and presenter of CAEL workshops.

Ernest G. Palola has been conducting research on the social organization of higher education for twenty years, and has published on individualized education, learning outcomes, educational and organizational evaluation, stress management, and national planning. He organized the Office of Research and Evaluation at Empire State College, an institution recognized for innovative approaches to learning services for adults. Currently he is organizing a research institute that will conduct studies on several themes important to professional-client relationships in adult development.

The environment surrounding the teaching/learning process contains norms important to encouraging sound learning outcomes. This chapter presents an account of the American Sociological Association's projects to institute a planned approach to the social change that influences learning outcomes.

Social Change and Learning Outcomes: A Planned Approach

Hans O. Mauksch

Outcome-oriented education cannot occur in a vacuum. It requires the ability of the teacher to establish a quasi-contractual relationship with the student in which control of the educational events, the organization of subject matter, and pedagogy are the ingredients of the contract. Much of the literature on learning outcomes treats the teaching/learning interaction as if mere commitment and effort by teachers could achieve the desired effects. Nothing could be further from the truth, however.

Many studies show that the student's involvement in the learning process is profoundly influenced by such variables as societal and group norms, the behavior patterns expected within the student culture of any given school, and the social pressures, fashions, and concerns characteristic of any given era, locality, or social stratum (Boocock, 1972; Cohen, 1972). Much less attention has been given to factors that enable or hinder the teacher in making a commitment towards systematic and outcome-oriented teaching (Blank, 1978; Blau, 1973). Indeed, the teacher is frequently portrayed as the sole originator of the teaching activities—as the independent variable in the teaching process (McGee, 1974; Solomon, Rosenberg, and Bezdek, 1964). It can be argued that, to a significant, indeed, to a crucial, degree, the teacher's performance, behavior, and orientation are the products of contextual forces and conditions (Goldsmid and Wilson, 1980; McGee, 1971). Teacher performance and the teaching process can be viewed as dependent variables, with institutional, disciplinary, and societal forces as independent variables.

The relationship between teacher effectiveness and contextual factors will be the theme of this chapter, even though its topical content will be devoted primarily to the efforts by one disciplinary association to influence and improve the conditions under which teachers conduct their craft. Ultimately, this chapter presents the claim that there are causal links between the details of classroom processes and the far distant behavior of national societies. The clarity and quality of learning outcomes that students experience in the classroom of our society are subtly, but significantly, related to the degree to which disciplinary associations identify instruction as one of the main agenda.

The relationship of disciplinary associations to the teaching function of their members has, at best, been an uneven one. Most disciplinary associations have traditionally functioned as societies of knowledge producers, scholars, and researchers. The well-being of the discipline has generally taken precedence over its application. Even the rather sparse attempts of some associations to concern themselves with the educational process have frequently been directed towards the training of future members of the discipline. The concern of such associations has been with the process of intellectual reproduction. The use of the discipline as an integral component of liberal learning and general education has had a mixed reception among various disciplines. Although the liberal arts function has been a focus of discussion within many of the humanities and, at least intermittently, a serious endeavor among the biological sciences, it has received hardly any attention from some of the social sciences.

Efforts on behalf of improvement of the teaching process by disciplinary associations have been directed towards various focal points and have had a range of different programmatic orientations. Among the most noteworthy ones have been those in which the disciplinary association has assumed responsibility for addressing the undergraduate curriculum, particularly in the case of physics, mathematics, and biology. With the help of sizable grants by the National Science Foundation (NSF), these disciplines have sponsored task forces that developed and proposed carefully restructured versions of the undergraduate curriculum in their respective disciplines. These programs, mainly conducted during the 1960s, have had demonstrable impact on the teaching and the program in these disciplines. One could characterize these programs as being primarily efforts to improve the organization, structure, and packaging of subject matter. Although assistance to teachers is part of the NSF-sponsored programs, they have primarily centered on the curriculum and its components.

Some disciplinary associations have sought to improve the educational process by facilitating access to recently developed or particularly significant areas of knowledge within the discipline. Geography and economics are disciplines in which significant projects have resulted in reports summarizing and facilitating selected segments of knowledge and subject matter. Sometimes associated with conferences or seminars, these efforts represent additions to the resources available to teachers.

Quite different from the programs that address teaching content are those that focus directly on the teacher. One can distinguish between those programs that seek to improve the teacher's competence in subject matter and those that address teaching skills, methods, tactics, and strategies. Some, such as one of the programs of the American Political Science Association, combine these two target areas. Several of the biological sciences and chemistry have a tradition of offering opportunities, for those who primarily teach, to update their knowledge, and to maintain and to improve their level of substantive competence.

The focus of this chapter is a program through which the American Sociological Association (ASA) sought to alter the conditions of teaching undergraduate sociology. Probably the basic assumption underlying the ASA Projects on Teaching Undergraduate Sociology is the view that the performance of any task is linked to certain sociopsychological and cultural factors. The act of teaching is therefore influenced by the way the actor feels about him or herself, the task to be performed, the degree to which the task is viewed as significant, worthy, and deserving of reward by significant others. Thus, teaching is directly affected by the availability of resources, support, and facilitation. The plans of the ASA projects were based on the conviction that the quality of teaching is not merely an expression of the teacher's competence and skills but is a direct product of the social status of teaching, the resources accorded to teachers, and the sense of worthiness associated with the teacher's role.

Because of these beliefs, the small group that in 1974 developed the proposal for the Projects on Teaching Undergraduate Sociology chose a pluralistic and admittedly complex approach. Beginning in the late 60s, several groups within the ASA had expressed concern with the quality of undergraduate sociology instruction. This concern with the quality of teaching was paralleled by claims that the ASA was not paying enough heed to teachers and was not sensitive to those sociologists who were working in small or isolated institutions. The Council of the ASA discussed this concern during several meetings between 1968 and 1971. During that period, a group of volunteers proposed the formation of a section on undergraduate education as one of the specialty segments within the ASA's structure. This proposal, having received sufficient signatures, was approved by the ASA Council in 1970.

A conference by the officers and council of the new section was held in Chicago in the fall of 1973. Substantive programmatic developments, it was agreed, would need to address the issue of teachers as well as content. Thus, it was decided that one programmatic direction needed to address the content, format, and organization of sociology courses and the process by which courses add up to a curriculum, be it for majors, minors, or for the liberal arts student.

While the educational literature is replete with this point of view, the designers of the ASA projects had to plan a curriculum that would be more than an assembly of courses and courses that would be more than mere presentation of content. One of the criteria for assessing a curriculum, according to the Chicago conference, was the principle that it had to be guided by explicit objectives. A curriculum was to be judged deficient if objectives were not stated in such a way that learning outcomes could be clearly communicated to the students and thus become the basis for evaluation.

Beyond the concern for the definition of what a curriculum and course represent, the ASA projects also had to address the structure and hierarchy of sociology. Some disciplines, notably mathematics, have a content structure that seems to require a progression from basic to more complex content; other disciplines give the impression that most of their content can be sorted horizontally without inherent requirements for increased complexity and advanced levels of conceptual substance. Sociology has been typically identified with the latter category; curriculum improvement, therefore, would have to address curriculum depth even more than curriculum breadth.

The second thrust was faculty development, including both teacher competence and teacher morale. At the time of the 1973 conference, this particular concern remained at the general level of articulation. Participants recognized that the teacher's sense of worth is as important as his or her command over the technology of teaching. As will be seen, this concern was subsequently much refined and developed into several programmatic directions.

The third concern discussed at the Chicago conference subsequently developed into an innovative approach regarding teaching. While those interested in curriculum improvement and faculty development could draw on the rich literature of education and psychology, there had been little attention paid to the institutional and cultural determinants of classroom processes. Using the basic precept of sociology that behavior is rooted in social structure and social process, those interested in the area of the structure of teaching invoked sociology by aiming at the social context within which teaching takes place. This context was identified, on the one hand, as the discipline—the nature, structure, and program of its organization and the degree to which it provides support, dignity, and services to the teacher. The impact of the discipline and its organizations can be positive but can also be negative if they discourage, deter, or frustrate the teacher. On the other hand, the teacher's context is defined by the institutions in which he or she is employed. Status and position, resources and rewards, policies and facilities all affect the meaning within which the teaching process becomes reality. At the intersection of the disciplinary forces and their institutional context is the teacher's departmental unit, which, in various fashions, structures the immediate environment and reflects the messages that affect the quality of teaching.

The Chicago discussions also acknowledged a fourth concern—the social factors that influence the student. The values, sanctions, priorities, and fashions that can be identified for each institution do not only influence teachers but place student behavior in a normative pressure system in which learning itself assumes widely differing value positions. Without acknowledging the importance of student background, student objectives, and student norms, learning outcomes are seen as the direct product of teacher objectives and curriculum content. In fact, however, learning outcomes are a synthesis of teacher intent and student response. Although there was general agreement about the importance of this fourth concern, everyone was aware that programming the student dimension required different resources and plans from those needed to address the first three factors.

The 1973 Chicago conference paid off handsomely. Early in 1974, the opportunity arose for a proposal to be submitted to the Fund for the Improvement of Postsecondary Education (FIPSE). In designing a proposal, the authors of the ASA projects had to consider the issues of resources, methodology, and feasibility. The distinct requirements of the fourth area of concern—the social factors influencing the student—made it necessary to omit this particular area from the proposal. Even at that, foundation officials and professional colleagues defined the proposed projects as unusually ambitious and complex. Three distinct groups of activities were proposed and individuals, institutions, associations, and the literature were all addressed simultaneously. The ASA Projects on Teaching Undergraduate Sociology were approved by FIPSE and began operating on September 1, 1974.

While the Chicago conference provided a general framework, the designers of the projects had to confront the choice of specific activities and tactics. Basing their plan on the contextual model of teacher performance, they opted to employ several methodologies simultaneously. They translated into action the premise that any complex system that rests on the balance between several components can only rarely be altered by addressing only one of the components.

All institutions, particularly those with professional staff, represent balance patterns of formal and informal power and status constellations.

Institutional and occupational conservatism frequently reflects reluctance to risk disturbing such a delicately balanced system rather than a resistance to change itself. Thus, designers of the projects recognized that teachers would not feel the most brilliantly conceived curriculum as their own product unless teachers were involved. The designers also recognized that, if postsecondary teachers feel their teaching is neither supported nor rewarded, the dissemination of additional skills and resources will merely heighten their frustration and sharpen their sense of impotence.

The projects sought to address the teacher's disciplinary context by planning activities designed to affect the structure and programs of the various disciplinary associations in sociology on the national, regional, and state levels. At the same time, the projects addressed the teacher's institutional context with programs designed to bring support for teaching activities into departments and to influence institutional administrators. Accompanied by these system-oriented activities, workshops and programs for the individual teacher could then address the teacher's skills and resources and, above all, his or her sense that teaching is important and significant.

The project leaders also chose pluralistic approaches to programs. Possibly one of the most significant choices and one that deserves study as a model for other activities was the decision to attempt to affect the normative climate. Without changes in norms and values, even the best activities and materials would have no lasting impact. In this, as in many other aspects of this project design, the classic study by Gunnar Myrdal, *An American Dilemma* (1944), served as model. What Myrdal had said about norms governing how people ought to feel and express themselves about blacks provided a clear parallel to the symbolic conditions that had to be faced by the ASA Projects on Teaching Undergraduate Sociology with respect to the norms about teaching.

The normative climate as identified in 1974 included a general expectation in academic circles, particularly in large universities, that teaching was not a subject worth discussing in detail. It was not seen as achieved competence or as deserving of reward but as a mere "lip service" component of the normal promotion and salary scheme. Universities expected that teaching would not take time away from those scholarly activities that were held to be the primary mission of the faculty member. This condition still prevails. To be sure, this normative climate varied according to the type and size of the institution; but, even in colleges overtly committed to teaching, the actual teaching performance and the teaching process were seldom topics of serious discussion or evaluation. Using a mixture of persuasion, documentation, and public relations techniques, the Projects on Teaching Undergraduate Sociology teams sought to address the issue of teaching recognition and worthiness as an integral part of their efforts. Activities included the frequent placement of stories and reports in *Footnotes,* the monthly ASA membership publication. The directors of the project also regularly sent letters to chairs, deans, and presidents, expressing the expectation that recognition be given to those devoting efforts towards teaching excellence. The importance of developing a supportive climate permeated all activities and became an integral part of all programs—even those primarily technical in nature.

It does not take much imagination to see that the normative climate of an institution is not confined to teachers and administrators. If the educational experience is emphasized, the distinction has to be made between the acceptance of clearly agreed upon learning outcomes and the mere processing of students through degree requirements. To accomplish consensus on outcomes, both faculty and students must experience an institutional climate that values and supports the teaching process for its achievement and significance rather than its efficiency and cost effectiveness.

The second type of project activity involved developing, collecting, and distributing materials and resources. Such activities were obviously much more tangible and concrete than the concern with normative climates. While the usual sociological publications, like those of most disciplines, provided continuous information about substantive and scientific developments in the discipline, very little space was devoted to issues of teaching. There had been little serious query about how to package and synthesize new knowledge for purposes of instruction. A teaching resource facility was needed to gather and make available a collection of those materials existing within the discipline. Those working with this facility would search in the literature of those disciplines that concentrate on the teaching/learning process—notably, education and psychology.

An observation is in order. Academics in each discipline or profession tend to be reluctant to acknowledge the products of another discipline. This attitudinal climate is particularly strong in the field of education. For complex and fascinating reasons, this discipline has been stigmatized by colleagues in other fields who thereby deprive themselves of its resources—a particularly regrettable isolation, since all disciplines are necessarily concerned with teaching. While the substantive, conceptual, and methodological characteristics of disciplines justify a degree of analytic separation, the intellectual and pedagogic issues of teaching cut across all disciplines. Teaching should be a basis for uniting educators from all fields and should lead to a sharing of resources. The leaders of the ASA projects discovered, however, that materials that originated in other fields became acceptable and widely used when they were sponsored and interpreted by sociologists and packaged and distributed by the ASA.

The third area of activities in the projects as outlined in the original design included workshops, departmental visitations, presentations, conferences, and consultation. At least as important as these programs themselves was the organizational strategy by which they were developed. The authors of the proposal claimed from the beginning that the feasibility of inducing change would be linked to the involvement of various kinds of teachers themselves. Sociologists solicited as volunteer participants were organized into small task groups, geographically proximate, and located in various areas across the United States. Each task group had as its mission one of the three thrusts (curriculum, teacher development, and institutional context).

By the spring of 1975, projects activities included 140 volunteers. Except for the director, the evaluator, and a small, part-time administrative staff, all participants donated their time. The six-year history of the ASA Projects on Teaching Undergraduate Sociology offers impressive testimony to the availability of voluntary participation for a cause that is stimulating and believed to be significant. The volunteer arrangement that originally achieved an optimum dissemination of change-oriented programs has in turn led to institutional absorption and transfer of responsibility to permanent functionaries.

The first two years of work were primarily devoted to the tasks assigned to each group. In the case of the curriculum task group, sub-task groups explored the issues of curriculum objectives in sociology. Each of the missions listed below was the responsibility of two sub-task groups:

1. Formulating objectives and the relationship of objectives to evaluation;
2. progression within the curriculum;
3. the boundary of sociology concerns;
4. concepts central to the teaching of sociology;
5. the function and organization of the first course in sociology;
6. the packaging of learning units or modules.

These sub-task groups developed materials, communicated with colleagues in their geographic vicinities, and, most importantly, developed competence and experience as resource personnel.

The teacher development task group operated very differently: Recognizing that the provision of materials and concepts would not be sufficient to alter teacher behavior and attitudes, the group decided to be more ambitious. It submitted a teacher development project to the Lilly Endowment. With the resources provided by this new grant, the group developed workshops for teachers and launched departmental visitation programs. Beyond serving the specific mission of this group, these programs soon became an outlet for the entire range of ASA project efforts. One outlet for the work of the various sub-task groups ultimately became the Teaching Resources Center, the first project component that could be transferred to a permanent, institutionalized home. The center found such a home in the Executive Office of the ASA in August 1978.

The number of organizations willing to sponsor funded projects is significantly larger than the number willing and able to absorb the product of this project into their permanent structure, however. Conversely, many project directors intend to create a permanent program but, in quasi-parental fashion, discover that they cannot let their offspring leave the nest. These two obstacles are of particular importance when one considers that it may take an intended audience a long time to trust a program's legitimacy and sincerity. Projects that endure only through the lifetime of the grant run the risk of raising hopes that are then betrayed and abandoned: A short-lived success may benefit the project director more than the recipients of services. Continuity and client expectations are the moral dimension of project management.

One of the key features of the ASA projects involved the goal of developing programs that would become permanent features of the ASA's programs. From the point of view of the teaching sociologist, the services of the ASA projects were always conveyed as being closely linked to the sponsoring organization, so that the transition, when it occurred, would be natural and expected.

Many of the programs that have now become part of ASA's permanent teaching services were first tested and developed within the framework of the teacher development project and the combined financial support of FIPSE and the Lilly Endowment. Workshops, departmental visitation programs, work with the state and regional societies, and the emergence of a teacher information exchange were made possible by channeling diverse initiatives into the enhanced capabilities of the project, which provided the opportunity to implement and test these ideas.

The third task group was concerned with institutional context. There is remarkably little existing literature on environmental, institutional, and subcultural approaches to the teaching process. The third task group, therefore, sought to conceptualize the various contexts that affect teaching.

One issue they explored was the process by which the skills, behaviors, and self-image of teachers is acquired—the processes and sources of formative factors. The typical graduate school is an environment that rewards those who pursue scholarship. Graduate curricula concentrate on training for research, with rarely a gesture toward possible application of this knowledge in the classroom. Promising future researchers receive—somewhat ironically—teaching assistantships. They are expected to muddle through their classes without formal training or even informal encouragement. A teaching assistantship is generally less prestigious than a research assistantship. Should one of this select company announce to the major dissertation advisor that he or she has made a career decision and has chosen undergraduate teaching at a liberal arts college, the senior professor would, in most instances, consider the student and himself a failure.

This environmental pressure is intensified by the prevailing myths about teaching. While research and scholarship involve skills that are attained laboriously, teaching is thought to be the product of native talent.

Competence in teaching, however, represents a range of knowledge and skills that can only be learned through hard work, however great one's native gifts. Not all teachers are virtuosos; even the master teacher lives unappreciated in the shadows. Teachers are thus socialized to think of themselves as second-class citizens before they ever enter their professional roles.

Once within the institutional context, teachers receive the messages associated with employment in a college or university: "You get hired to teach, but you get raises, promotion, and tenure for anything else but teaching" (verbatim comment from a questionnaire received by the task group on institutional context). College campuses reflect the expectation that everyone can teach, that this should be taken for granted, and that faculty rewards should therefore be based on other criteria, such as publications.

Beyond the messages and arrangements surrounding employment are actual institutional resources. Universities and colleges often invest less in the physical appearance, convenience, and pedagogical appropriateness of classrooms than they do in furnishing administrative offices, social facilities, and athletic fields. While there are some notable exceptions, many teachers who wish to use audiovisual resources must ferret them out of inconvenient storage facilities and drag them to inconveniently situated classrooms. Within the departmental domain, the allocation of space and the location of offices impart the message of a status system in which those who teach basic courses and those who are primarily teachers rank lowest.

Most deprived or low status groups come to perceive the doling out of resources as an award rather than an entitlement. Whether this applies to secretarial services, an acceptable classroom, an adequate office, a telephone, or funds to attend a teaching workshop, institutional resource management and allocation have much more direct impact on the classroom than institutional business managers usually understand.

The conceptual work done by the task group on institutional context raises fundamental issues that relate the teaching environment to the teaching process. Teachers do indeed convey much more in what they say and do than the mere subject matter. The teacher who feels the need to protect a threatened status may demonstrate what Goffman (1961, p. 85) has aptly called role distance, by conveying that he or she has "other fish to fry" and that teaching this course is just a distasteful obligation. Such verbal and nonverbal behavior will seriously affect, indeed negate, any attempt to say the right words about objectives and learning outcomes. While clarifying learning outcomes is generally thought to be a form of teacher/student contract, it is also a risk-taking activity, in which teachers may feel increased vulnerability to sanctions from superordinates who control raises, promotions, and resources. Developing a semester plan and long-range efforts and permitting student challenge and clarification require that a teacher feel firm institutional support and trust.

These were the considerations that the ASA projects had to confront. The projects had the opportunity to reach sociology teachers directly by offering programs and material. Teachers response to these activities would show whether they were willing to become involved—whether the programs offered met their needs and gained their confidence. Influencing disciplinary associations and affecting their structure, programs, and prevailing norms were much more difficult and elusive missions that involved creating high visibility, developing a constituency, and enhancing influence. Yet the disciplinary associations were much easier to impact than the campuses themselves.

Educational institutions are, in a sense, a federation of disciplinary islands that compete with each other for influence and are more likely to emphasize their divergent interests than to consolidate around common goals. No one discipline, however dynamically it has been renewed, can be presumptuous enough to expect that it can alter institutional conditions all by itself. Changing institutional environments for teachers ultimately requires cross-disciplinary cooperation and the recognition that teaching is a serious, scholarly activity that unites all professors and transcends disciplinary and departmental divisions. The ASA projects have made modest gains towards this objective.

Funding from FIPSE terminated in July, 1979. The grant from Lilly Endowment supported the teacher development project through January, 1981. Many programs have now been incorporated into the permanent operations of the ASA. Others continue to function under the aegis of the projects.

The aims of the projects have necessarily included changes in the structure, program, and norms of the disciplinary association. Conditions have been favorable, since it is much more acceptable to neglect teaching than to actively oppose it. The support for the projects from ASA officers and staff has been genuine and enthusiastic. The projects proved a convenient enterprise, since they helped take the heat off ASA official bodies whenever issues of teaching and support for teachers were raised. Such factors helped in the beginning. Crucial leverage for further success was provided by the documented response by teachers to workshops and other project programs. With almost every program oversubscribed and with myriad letters of support and appreciation, the project leadership was able to translate educational achievement into political currency.

The most immediate result of this process can be seen in the ASA annual convention programs of the last ten years. Sessions devoted to teaching and related topics were scarce until 1974, but they have increased dramatically in the years since then. This recalls Myrdal's (1944, pp. 75–78) description of social change as a spiral of "cumulative causation." By the summer of 1978, the ASA was ready to incorporate the Teaching Resources Center into its own Executive Office. In 1979, the ASA Council committed themselves to a teaching services program, and, in the spring of 1980, ASA Council approved its first budget. Meanwhile, project activities had catapulted several individuals into prominence, creating the beginning of a network with possible ballot power. Indeed, some members of this teaching-based network have since been elected to office and named to committees.

While influencing the ASA was crucial to long-range acceptance and survival, the heart of the projects is their teacher-oriented programs. Although the various programs are listed below, it is impossible to capture the nuances of change and development that occurred as, in each instance, there were conscious attempts to learn from the constituency, to modify, and to respond.

The Teaching Resources Center. This facility, begun tentatively with programs from the various task groups and materials from sociology and other disciplines, has met with overwhelming response. One third of the currently available materials originated outside the field of sociology. The sixty-item list includes project monographs ranging from reports on surveys of sociology departments to a guidebook on teaching basic sociological concepts. It includes bibliographies, resource listings, and sets of sample syllabuses.

Three lessons can be learned from this experience. Most importantly, this enterprise demonstrated that teachers will expend effort and money to buy materials in support of teaching—if teaching itself is legitimated and if materials are made accessible and distributed in a context of enthusiasm. Five to six thousand items per year can add up to a significant impact in such a setting. The second lesson, already mentioned, is that many of these materials would not normally have been seen by sociologists. Sponsorship by a disciplinary association helps transcend interdisciplinary resistance. Even in workshops, the response to these materials has been uniformly positive; but this has only been true when they have been presented and discussed by sociologists. The third lesson came from the ease with which the ASA Executive Office included material from other disciplines among the items it distributed. Assuming and expecting cooperation is frequently a major step towards success. Interdisciplinary rivalries are real, but they need not be aggravated; indeed, they can be diminished with approaches that assure and facilitate cooperative response.

The Teaching Resources Center is directed by an ASA staff member and guided by an advisory committee. New products are continuously solicited and selected, and the lively response from the teaching community keeps this operation extremely busy.

Workshops. Aided by the support from the Lilly Endowment, the teacher development task group was the first to develop workshops. Subsequently, workshops were also conducted by both the curriculum and the institutional context task groups. Most workshops have been directed to teachers, and workshop objectives have never been restricted to information transfer or even to skill development. They have always included developing informal teacher networks and exploring the sociopsychological dimensions of the teacher's role.

Early workshops usually focused on content organization, the use of objectives, approaches to evaluation, and the relationship between sociology topics and teaching options. There was also some discussion of role requirements, teacher assertiveness, and strategies for obtaining resources. Though they were intensive, they included time for colleague exchange. Over 1,000 sociology teachers participated in these workshops, each of which was oversubscribed. During the last two years, workshops for teachers have developed a more specialized format. Thus, in the fall of 1980, one was specifically geared to course and curriculum development and a second addressed faculty and student evaluation.

Other workshops are not directed to teachers. Several have been aimed at helping to prepare future teachers, requiring each institution to send at least one doctoral program faculty member and one graduate student. These workshops explored the graduate curriculum as a setting for teacher development, education opportunities for teaching assistants, and the informal climate of graduate schools with regard to teaching. Every session has been filled, a somewhat surprising response. The task group on institutional context also offered two workshops for departmental chairs, addressing the administrative and departmental conditions that enable teachers to be motivated, to feel rewarded, and to make their relationships with students a priority of their professional life.

A series of workshops conducted in the spring of 1980 demonstrate the symbolic utilization of a program. Ten simultaneous workshops were announced for one April weekend in localities covering the entire country. At the same time, the ASA proclaimed April as Teaching Month. In ASA *Footnotes* and a specially designed brochure, departments were encouraged to plan special activities and consider sending someone to one of the workshops. This approach enhanced the impact of these workshops considerably beyond those who attended. A similar series is planned for the spring of 1981.

The workshop program has been transferred successfully as well and is now part of the ASA Teaching Services Program.

Departmental Visitation Program. While addressing individual teachers through workshops, the ASA projects also developed a departmental visitation program. This program was seen as an important vehicle for influencing the institutional context both within and beyond the sociology department.

The first step was developing a teaching resources group (TRG). It was recruited from volunteers who had acquired experience and competence in selected areas of instructional concerns, such as faculty development, faculty or student evaluation, course or curriculum planning, the first sociology course, and effective relationships with students. This group also worked on achieving a common level of resource skills, such as consulting techniques, assisting groups in clarifying issues and achieving decisions, and in relating teaching topics to departmental management. This service was publicized in ASA *Footnotes* in 1977, and, since then, over sixty institutions including universities, four-year colleges, and community colleges have requested and received TRG visits. Visitations have been uniformly well received and invitations keep coming in. During the last year a number of visitations have involved not only the sociology faculty but the entire institutional teaching staff. These visits have been particularly gratifying, as they have helped faculty from widely different disciplines develop a sense of common interest and commitment.

The departmental visitation program has offered important lessons. First, the resource person is less an expert who imparts wisdom than an informed outsider who legitimates discussion in the institutions' collective search for new solutions. It seems that the visiting expert creates an audience that applauds and remains outside, while the visiting colleague creates a working group that participates and continues its work after the visitor has withdrawn.

The visitation program has been absorbed by the ASA Teaching Services Program. Its operation is managed by a volunteer coordinator with modest support from the ASA.

Service to Sociological Societies. Another project function that has become part of the ASA Teaching Services Program is a set of activities designed to assist sociological societies. In addition to the ASA, there are eight regional and approximately thirty-two state societies. Since 1975, the project staff has participated in the programs of almost all of these organizations and, in the case of state societies, has frequently assumed major responsibility for annual programs and special events. Since teachers from small and/or rural colleges are frequently limited to attending state meetings, involvement in state societies has extended the reach of project programs to a new constituency. Service includes program participation as well as display and other materials from the Teaching Resources Center.

Teacher Information Exchange. One of the more recent project developments, this activity will only be incorporated into the regular ASA program when it has been developed and tested. It makes a panel of volunteers available, through a telephone network, to offer advice and information to teachers of sociology. Volunteers include specialists in various frequently taught courses, and in teaching resources, methodologies, and techniques. This program has been functioning for one year, and although the beginnings are very promising, its long-range effectiveness cannot yet be assessed.

Scholarly Research on Teaching. Since the projects sought to change norms, status, and levels of respect regarding teaching, efforts have not been limited only to symbolic statements and developing the skills of the individual teacher. The projects had, in addition, to address the level of written and oral discourse about teaching within the profession. This was particularly important for sociology, which has a great deal to contribute to our knowledge about teaching as a social process and the classroom as a social structure. The projects sponsored several monographs currently distributed by the Teaching Resources Center (see, for example, Baker and Wilson, 1979; Geertsen and others, 1979) and a recent book is closely linked to the project programs (Goldsmid and Wilson, 1980). Three special issues of *Teaching Sociology*—April 1976, October 1977, and April 1980—and the February 1980 issue of *The American Sociologist* have also been devoted to articles by project participants.

All too frequently, academics think of teaching and research as opposites. A fundamental argument of the ASA projects is that both can be done in a scholarly fashion. Either can be performed with intellectual sophistication just as either can be done in a technical or bureaucratic way. The link between teaching and scholarship needs not only to be asserted but also demonstrated.

This emphasis on defining teaching as a scholarly activity applies not only to reports about teaching but to teaching itself. The very definition of learning outcomes implies a rigorous intellectual system in which results are linked to the management of planned variables.

Summary

Describing these programs was not intended as a mere listing of distinct activities. The complexity of design of the ASA Projects on Teaching Undergraduate Sociology was described in these pages to present an argument for planned approaches to social change and a scenario that is deemed essential for achieving conditions of practice in which teachers can arise to their intellectual and professional peak. It should be noted that one of the most pernicious by-products of socialization into minority group status tends to be the internalized acceptance of low worth, lack of power, and the acceptance of social limits. Whether it be the history of blacks, of women, of workers, or of teachers, minority socialization prevents the development of a sense of assertive self-reliance and proud assumption of control. It is well known that students do not only hear what teachers say but can sense how teachers feel about their role and function. Control over conditions of practice, access to appropriate resources, and the respect earned for being a teacher are basic ingredients as important to quality teaching as are command of the subject matter and techniques of presentation.

If one accepts that the prevailing condition in postsecondary education provides sociopsychological and structural restraints on quality teaching, conditions for change need to be examined. The ASA Projects on Teaching Undergraduate Sociology represent an attempt to create change by simultaneously seeking to modify several components of a social system. Addressing the teacher had to be accompanied by behaviors that conveyed to the teacher that the system was being moved and that there was strength in a common set of interests and a network of communications.

To be a teacher is a consequential social role. To affect the minds and attitudes of future generations should be a task performed by individuals conveying strength and commitment. The lessons learned by sociologists during the last few years add up to several recommendations that sound simple, should be simple, but that are, in fact, achievable only by concerted effort and courage. To bring to teaching the willingness to take risks cannot be achieved by isolated individuals. Within departments and, more importantly, within entire educational institutions, faculty need to discover that they have common interests and common concerns based on their role as teachers. These bases for communication and for concerted action may differ from faculty alignments as researchers and as disciplinarians. The legitimacy of the teaching community and its professional function as a platform for quality must be established. Yet, this cannot be achieved without an attack on the norm that teaching competence is innate and that it, therefore, need not be rewarded or be subject to hard and deliberate work.

These recommendations lead to others. Teaching and teaching performance must come out of the closet. As long as it is deemed a wholly private activity, teaching cannot really claim to be an accountable professional function. Like all other scholarly pursuits, teaching must be open and subject to peer participation. Among the most impressive experiences of the last four years has been the sense of excitement with which teachers from many disciplines participated in collective teaching clinics. They frequently entered the clinics with trepidation based on the dread of an embarrassing self-exposure. Yet these clinics have turned out to be a unifying experience, in which the craft of teaching became a bond across departments, across disciplines, even across profoundly different styles of presentation.

The preceding pages record the efforts of one discipline to alter the conditions of teaching and the status of the teacher. Permeating all of the reported efforts to change the context of teaching was the belief in the comprehensiveness and interdependence of the human experience. Devoting scholarly commitment and rigor to the attainment of demonstrable learning outcomes is more likely linked to a teacher's sense of worthiness and institutional support than to imposed requirements and contractual obligations. Although this volume is primarily concerned with the clarification of learning outcomes, this process must be linked to the recognition that even such demonstrably desirable behaviors will only become part of the teacher's regular repertory if the objectives and the process of their definition are consistent with the teacher's total experience.

References

American Sociologist, 1980, *15* (1).

Baker, P. J., and Wilson, E. (Eds.). *KAKN: Knowledge Available and Knowledge Needed to Improve Instruction in Sociology*. Washington, D.C.: ASA, 1979.

Blank, R. "An Organizational Model of Higher Education, Institutions, and Faculty Teaching Goals." *Sociological Inquiry*, 1978, *48* (1), 23-25.

Blau, P. M. *The Organization of Academic Work*. New York: Wiley, 1973.

Boocock, S. S. *An Introduction to the Sociology of Learning*. Boston: Houghton Mifflin, 1972.

Cohen, E. G. "Sociology and the Classroom: Setting the Conditions for Teacher-Student Interaction." *Review of Educational Research*, 1972, *42*, 44-52.

Geertsen, R., Sundeen, R., Allen, P., and Gunning, E. (Eds.). *Eighty-One Techniques for Teaching Sociological Concepts*. Washington, D.C.: ASA, 1979.

Goffman, E. *Encounters*. Indianapolis, Ind.: Bobbs-Merrill, 1961.

Goldsmid, C. A., and Wilson, E. K. *Passing On Sociology: The Teaching of a Discipline*. Belmont, Calif.: Wadsworth, 1980.

McGee, R. *Academic Janus: The Private College and Its Faculty*. San Francisco: Jossey-Bass, 1971.

McGee, R. "Does Teaching Make Any Difference?" *Teaching Sociology*, 1974, *1* (2), 210-223.

Myrdal, G. *The American Dilemma*. New York: Harper & Row, 1944.

Solomon, D., Rosenberg, L., and Bezdek, W. E. "Teacher Behavior and Student Learning." *Journal of Educational Psychology*, 1964, *55* (1), 23-30.

Teaching Sociology, 1976, *3* (3); 1977, *5* (1); 1980, *7* (3).

Hans O. Mauksch is professor of sociology and professor of family and community medicine at the University of Missouri, Columbia, Missouri. In 1974 he became director of the Projects on Teaching Undergraduate Sociology of the American Sociological Association (ASA). He has directed this national program while serving two years as ASA executive officer. He also serves as coordinator of the ASA Workshop and Departmental Visitation Program. He has worked with individual sociologists, departments and colleges, and professional societies on programs of teacher development.

The current faculty role is influenced by two philosophical themes operating in higher education. By rethinking these antithetical perspectives and redefining the faculty role within higher education, faculty can strengthen learning outcomes.

Faculty Role in Clarifying Student Learning Outcomes

A. Paul Bradley, Jr.
Susan Olson Bolman

The coming years will be turbulent and potentially difficult for colleges and universities (Millett, 1977). Faculty will have a particularly difficult time maintaining their role as a result of recent changes in the larger society that have already had a significant impact on higher education. Many problems have emerged for which there has been relatively little preparation. The American Assembly, considering many facets of the times and the immediate future, including the integrity of higher education, concluded that higher education is in a state of confusion, evidencing no clear direction (Walton and Bolman, 1979). The twenty-five years after World War II were times of growth and relative stability for higher education. Then change multiplied in rapid fashion. Drucker (1980) indicates that the challenge for human organizations is to clearly define themselves, giving attention to mission and objectives. The reward for this activity will be prosperity, the price of failure, dissolution. Higher education, through its faculties, must accept this challenge.

This chapter examines the faculty role in higher education, pointing up the need for faculty to take hold of the specific challenge to reassess and reassert their role as professionals. Faculty must seize the opportunity to focus on the manipulation of educational content and process to achieve clearly defined learning outcomes for students. Faculty can make four types of contributions toward the clarification of outcomes. They can serve as individual forces, shapers, contributors, and extenders in various faculty arenas. Though two divergent philosophies within higher education are at work and often at odds with each other, faculty can reassert their role as professionals by clarifying their own philosophical stance with regard to these two particular opposing perspectives and working toward more deliberate learning outcomes.

The Historical Roots of the Faculty Role

Two antithetical themes with classical antecedents influence contemporary teaching and learning, here called the idealist and pragmatist schools of thought. The idealist school, which can be traced to Greek thought as found in Plato's academy—where truth was sought for its own sake and for preparing philosophers to be kings—has the broad objective of character formation (*paideia*). In contrast, the Sophists favored the teaching of rhetoric and acquisition of useful skills to attain success in life. Emphasizing its focus on application, we label this perspective pragmatist. Identification with one side or the other of this dichotomy (Brubacher and Rudy, 1958; Kerr, 1966; Veysey, 1965) informs the personal style and philosophic stance of individual faculty. To illuminate these viewpoints, we briefly trace their sources and identify forces encouraging and mitigating their influence.

During the colonial period, the eighteenth century, and for most of the nineteenth century, the American college was dominated by the idealist school. The curriculum, designed for gentlemen bound for the professions and clergy, was organized around the rigorous study of the classics. The Yale Faculty Report of 1828 was a benchmark of the period. It declared unequivocal support for traditionally prescribed classical studies and the recitative method, in which classes required a show of memory (Brubacher and Rudy, 1958). With the passage of the Morrill Act of 1862, however, land-grant universities were established. The resultant institutions came to stand for two ideas: the all-purpose curriculum and service to the needs of the community. Cornell University represented the former, while the University of Wisconsin epitomized the latter. Both broadened the concepts inherent in the faculty role. No longer was it appropriate for faculty simply to listen to recitation. A faculty member was expected to be an orator, an active learner, a curriculum developer, and a contributor to society. Further, given the greater diversity in students and the wide arrays of student educational aspirations, faculty found a need for active teaching. This expectation led to greater use of lecture as opposed to mere recitation (Veysey, 1965).

During the 1930s, a running debate took place between the two schools. The idealist champion, Robert Maynard Hutchins, opposed the increasing momentum of a democratized university, clearly identifying the function of the university as the development of intellectual knowledge (1936). A well-known Hutchins summary conveys his view neatly: "Education implies teaching. Teaching implies knowledge. Knowledge is truth. The truth is everywhere the same. Hence, education should be everywhere the same" (p. 66). "The aim of higher education is wisdom" (p. 98). To accomplish this, one must he said, engage the great books. Though there was no equality in the various areas of knowledge, a hierarchy existed in which practical studies were near the bottom. Thus, a faculty versed in the classics and capable of drawing out their truths was essential to fulfilling the mission of education.

John Dewey, a pragmatist proponent, took issue with the idea that the university was for conceptualization while practice was for the real world. Holders of this alternative view doubted whether people could learn anything apart from the context in which it was illustrated. Further, they felt that education must continuously undergo change to meet the changes in the environment. The faculty role, in Dewey's view, was one involving an articulation of the relationship between theory and practice (1937; 1938).

The Emergence of the Pragmatist School

Certain historical treatises on American higher education document a shift from the idealist to pragmatist view in the early nineteenth century (Brubacher and Rudy, 1958; Rudolph, 1962). In the 1940s, the faculty at Harvard tried to synthesize the two contrasting philosophies in a report entitled *General Education in a Free Society,* (1945)—often referred to as the Red Book. Educators across the country read and discussed this publication, though it failed by itself either to resolve the debate or to offer any clear blueprints. However, given the strength of the pragmatists at that time, the dispersal of articulate, cogent arguments on behalf of idealist concepts seemed to stimulate the latter viewpoint and served to energize the reawakening of that school.

The 1950s were a time of relative stability for faculty. After a large influx of students immediately following World War II, growth continued in a smooth, almost manageable fashion. Neither the idealist nor the pragmatist school was predominant. Some of the comfortable smugness of the times was shaken with the publication of Philip Jacob's *Changing Values in College* (1957). Jacob pointed out that American colleges and universities, with few exceptions, had little impact on student attitudes and values. Indeed, he found the main effect of college to be homogenization: Students simply became more like each other. While this report was not as widely discussed as the Red Book, it served equally well as a benchmark capturing the relative placidity of the 1950s. Studies subsequent to the Jacob report (Chickering, 1969; Katz, 1968; Sanford, 1962; Sanford, 1967), indicate similarly that even into the 1960s the faculty role was not clearly defined relative to student needs.

Forces Strengthening the Pragmatist Position. The launching of Sputnik in 1958 marked the beginning of an era in which the pragmatist view was notably strengthened. This historic event signaled attention to the concept of knowledge as power. Institutions of higher learning were subsequently urged to serve broader social ends. Practical knowledge was emphasized; egalitarianism with education as the vehicle became—even more than before—the force behind upward social mobility. Forces strengthening the pragmatist school included societal attitudes based on relevance, federal and state initiatives for service and equal opportunity, and pressures for student input into programs and policies.

Social attitudes influenced the pragmatist viewpoint by turning campus attention outward, making the university community an actor in real world events. The civil rights movement and the presidential candidacy of Eugene McCarthy moved many faculty into the community; Earth Day and the women's movement captured the spirit and morality of others. Shoben (1968) characterizes this new quality of faculty as a clash of intellectual styles; contrasted were the essentialist tradition and the existentialist. Under goals focused on relevance, authenticity, engagement, and credibility, pragmatist faculty opened the campus to include social, political, and human rights issues. Some issues spawned programs such as black and women's studies. Other issues gave rise to learning from sources beyond the bounds of the campus: junior year abroad, VISTA, and service-based internships. The outcome of these thematic and programmatic shifts was the need to question what indeed constituted relevance.

Along with the diverse effects of social issues, the more tangible influence of government was felt in the campus environment. The federal government's impact increased dramatically: The National Defense Education Act (1958) was a start toward the influx of massive federal support. This was followed by other major allocations for student aid and research (such as the National Science Foundation). But it was in the Higher Education Act of 1965 that the concept of a major federal role took root. This bill contained something for everyone: direct aid to developing institutions, libraries, facilities, students, and research. Much emphasis fell on programs more oriented toward immediate public benefit. The huge federal student aid programs (National Direct Student Loans, Basic and Supplementary Opportunity Grants, and College Work-Study) have made access to postsecondary study available to hundreds of thousands of students. State programs added still more incentive for college attendance. Under all this pressure, the idealists tried to continue their mission, agreeing that theirs was not an education for the masses, that mainstream Americans should have practical education leading to jobs. A conflict with deeply seated roots was set in motion.

Monies for cooperative education also enticed many institutions to sponsor learning opportunities that alternated study and work (Keeton and Tate, 1978). With students moving outside of the classroom, the teaching task was to draw connections between the theoretical and the practical. These programs clearly influenced faculty teaching styles. Cooperative education and experiential learning were forces supporting the pragmatist view.

An impressive array of research documents the movement of traditional educators toward experiential learning (Chickering, 1969; Katz, 1968; Sanford, 1962, 1967). Various foundations provided support for study on time-shortened degree alternatives, for the External Degree Program of the University of the State of New York, and for other departures from traditional paths. Several of these projects focused on adult audiences, seen as an important and growing clientele in the face of an imminent decline in students more traditionally aged (17 to 24). However, with adult students came a predictable interest in practical studies. In many cases, faculty found that the old ways of working with students no longer proved completely satisfactory. New approaches and teaching styles were developed (Bradley, 1975, 1978; Ralph and Freedman, 1973).

Another force strengthening the pragmatist position is student consumerism. The notion of student as consumer had its beginning in 1975, when the need to account for student aid funds stimulated the Federal Interagency Committee on Education to label the postsecondary student a consumer. A variety of mechanisms were proposed to protect students from misleading catalog statements and advertising at a time when many colleges and universities were beginning to be concerned about student enrollments. Students became aware that they could shop around for curricula meeting their personal as well as educational needs (Stark, Terenzini, and Trani, 1978). Similarly, colleges sought new consumers, namely foreign nationals. This constituency also forced changes in curricular offerings, such as more useful courses in business, social science, and other experientially based subjects.

As the 1970s ended, the Harvard faculty issued another report that underscored the pragmatist viewpoint as an increasing national trend. Whereas the Red Book report had concluded that general education focused on knowledge, the 1978 Harvard faculty *Report on General Education* suggested that general education included skills as well as knowledge.

The Weakening of the Idealist Position. Mass media, the increasing sophistication of students, the growing numbers of underprepared students, and the loss of faculty mobility have served to weaken the position of idealist faculty. The impact of mass media on higher education is still not fully understood and should be carefully studied. Our impressions are that several trends are emerging: Students are becoming oriented toward graphics, more impatient, and somewhat cynical. The slow pace of traditional lecture teaching methods is not only deemed uninteresting in comparison to the fast moving events depicted on television, but lecture material often seems irrelevant and trivial. Many students come from modern well-equipped secondary schools where they have been introduced to some of the material once considered the province of colleges. Not realizing the overlap, faculty often find that courses in introductory subjects seem "old hat" to students. Though we recognize that our teaching experience may not be representative, we find that many students have had extensive sensual experiences (such as drug-induced "trips") foreign to most professors and that once provocative eye-openers, such as the intricacies of Bertrand Russell, D. H. Lawrence, or Malthus seem quite tame by comparison. It appears to us that many students come to college less for an awakening than in response to societal expectations and the need for a credential.

Another force working against the elitist stance of idealist educators came in the form of open admissions. As a result of social pressures, higher education was increasingly seen as a right, not a privilege. While open access had been present for decades in some institutions, others were encouraged to examine admissions criteria and broaden their constituencies. Many students, not yet ready for higher level learning, were given a near assurance of receiving a degree (Bolman, 1979). Faculty voiced concerns about the ensuing pressure to ensure that all students passed courses. Large numbers of underprepared students proved demoralizing to faculty whose educational priorities and standards had focused on developing abstract concepts and analytical thought. A lack of basic skills, making more advanced learning almost impossible, further eroded the traditional mission.

Though once characterized as highly mobile (Brown, 1966; Caplow and McGee, 1958), faculty in recent years have had to confront both the realities and anxieties of a declining job market that imposes serious limitations on their mobility. While graduate schools continue to produce record numbers of new doctoral candidates, the number of positions has declined drastically, due to declining enrollments and financial pressures to disband programs. Institutional responses have included the setting of *de jure* and *de facto* tenure quotas. Further complicating the situation has been the advent of affirmative action in response to social pressure to open career pathways for women and blacks. While some positions were available, a widespread view was that they were "earmarked." One response to tenure quotas was the strengthening of faculty unions. Overall, the loss of mobility weakened the idealist objectives.

The loss of much autonomy in recent years poses a genuine threat to traditional notions of the faculty as professionals. In education, the following features are considered appropriate to the professional qualities of faculty: employment in a full-time position, a high degree of personal commitment to the position, and responsibilities requiring esoteric and useful skills and knowledge based on specialized training or education. The true professional operates in a service orientation, holding a keen perception of client need relative to his or her competence, attending to those client needs through competent performance. The professional enjoys relative autonomy, restrained by responsibility. Though these elements all are important, the latter attributes carry more weight in establishing professional status. The greater the individual freedom in the exercise of judgment, the higher the professional stature (Moore, 1970). As a result of erosion of the faculty role, professionals are facing reduction to semiprofessional status. This would have profound implications for the future of the academy itself.

In a real sense, the critical challenge for faculty in the 1980s is to reassert themselves—to define what it is that makes the faculty role special, whether in a classroom, as a member of a department, as part of an educational institution, or as a participant in some extramural organizational structure. We suggest that one thing that is special and unique to faculty is their expertise in and responsibility for identifying desired learning outcomes for students.

The Faculty Role Today

Faculty as Individual Forces. Faculty hold considerable potential as individuals to help students focus on outcomes. By developing a course or in preparation for a single class session, faculty can identify clear expectations for students and develop methods for eliciting appropriate responses. An idealist approach might stimulate the cognitive interaction of students with important concepts to activate their abstract thinking, in Wegener's words, to cultivate "the arts of disciplined purposive thought; the arts of the intellectual" (1978, p. 89). A pragmatist, on the other hand, might endeavor to have students grapple with realistic problems, aiming to facilitate the transference from conceptual learning to real life situations. Similarly, faculty as individual forces can serve as powerful models in the role of advisor. The idealist might strive to interest students in the life of the mind, in the satisfactions of intellectual mastery. The pragmatist might use sessions with a student to explore linkages between what the student has studied and his or her career aspirations. These approaches are in use in some manifestations of the faculty role (Bradley, 1974, 1978).

The gap between potential impact and reality is notable. Except in educational processes where results are expected by procedures and policies, faculty often give little attention to learning outcomes. The literature is replete with evidence of faculty repeatedly teaching the same courses with little change from year to year (see, for example, Gaff, 1975). Rather than developing unique approaches, faculty often emulate the style and substance of favorite graduate school professors. The typical pattern reveals faculty engaged in transmitting knowledge. Other aspects of Bloom's Taxonomy of Educational Objectives—comprehension, application, analysis, synthesis, evaluation—receive little attention (Bloom, 1956). Similarly, developmental objectives such as student understanding of self and others, awareness, openness, development of self-esteem, and clarification of purpose, receive no concentrated effort (Chickering, 1969). Such outcomes can emerge, but are seldom the result of design.

Recent reports give testimony to the fact that faculty as individuals can become significant forces when they engage in outcome-oriented teaching. We draw specific guidance from work developed by Mager (1962) and Barry (1978). Discussing instructional objectives, Mager stresses a common theme throughout: those who do not know where they are going are liable to end up elsewhere. Objectives describe an educational intent, showing what behavior to expect and how to identify achievement. Barry, using retrospective analysis of his twenty-five years as a teacher, found that he could characterize teaching and learning as active, positive processes. The challenge is to tell students what changes should take place in them during the course and then to structure the experience so that this can happen. Students who can monitor their own progress can understand better whether they are on the track. Barry concludes with the following precepts:

> 1. Instructors should write their own course objectives. None should be imposed from without though, naturally, all courses must be consistent with the requirements of a series of persons and groups (e.g. the Board, the department).
>
> 2. Instructors must develop course objectives in conjunction with the students. This permits student ownership of the course. Student participation occurs by reacting to instructor-presented objectives and by selecting alternative methods for implementing and attaining them.
>
> 3. At no time is it possible to have completed the development of objectives; the process is ongoing. While the teacher is trained, the process of teaching is not private; it is articulated to the students, thus involving them [1978, pp. 31–32].

Faculty likewise can serve forceful roles in the advising process, yet they frequently resent the perfunctory role they are expected to serve as approvers of courses selected for term registration. While the virtues of making students responsible for their own choices are many, so too are the virtues of serious conversations on the problem of selecting appropriate components toward a degree plan. At Northland College in Ashland, Wisconsin, the faculty role in student advisement was redefined. Calling the faculty *mentors*, Northland instituted a system of advisement for the 1975 incoming class that required regular follow-up after registration plus the administration of biographical research tools. Faculty did not see these advisement tasks as onerous; in fact they derived much personal satisfaction from the fact that attrition was lowered and students reported a clarified sense of direction. This experiment, expanded in subsequent years, stands as a clear example of how faculty as individual forces can help students clarify outcomes (Witthun, Kegel, and Haukaas, 1976).

Faculty as Shapers in a Department. Collectively, faculty can consider the outcomes of curricula and degree programs, as well as in advisement responsibilities for majors. Whether accomplished from an idealist or pragmatist stance, concerns for what is happening in cognitive areas can be identified by addressing several questions: What kinds of students does the department want to produce? What should graduates be able to do? What should graduates from the department know? What intellectual skills should graduates possess? What is the purpose of each course required or offered? Is there a defined reason for a course sequence? How do departmental courses (or the major) relate to the general (or core) curriculum?

A study by Dressel, Johnson, and Marcis (1971) found that most departmental curriculum committees used no systematic principles in reviewing existing or proposed courses. Among the pervasive problems identified were course proliferation, small classes, needless course repetition, and low-credit courses. Further, most departmental curricula had undergone little—if any—evaluation. In short, departmental curricula served as little more than an act of faith when scrutinized. While few departments face the need for sweeping changes, almost all could profit from periodic, systematic review of the rationale operating to produce the offerings of the department. Faculty can contribute significantly to this process by engaging in continuous assessment of how (and why) their courses contribute to curricula in meaningful ways.

Faculty as Contributors to Multidepartmental Groups. A strong campus-wide group with coherent policies focused on institutional and student outcomes can exert a major influence on the way individuals and departments approach learning outcomes. For example, an idealist committee can raise questions about how students will be asked to deal with logical or analytical problems. A pragmatist committee might expect a clear statement of how a body of content or a learning mode (such as an internship or field work) contributes to career preparation. Multidepartmental committees can serve the institution well by provoking curricular justifications. An example of faculty-initiated self-examination is the complete restructuring of the curriculum conducted at Worcester Polytechnic Institute. Students must now define personal objectives and take responsibility for learning outcomes. The success of the approach proves that faculty can take hold of its role, encouraging meaningful activities that address learning outcomes (for additional comments on this program, see the chapter by Harrisberger in the present volume).

Faculty as Extenders in Multi-Institutional Settings. Still another arena where faculty can play an important role is in activities beyond the bounds of their institution—through participation in disciplinary association activities focused on outcome concerns and in academic consortia. A particularly good example of a discipline-wide activity addressing teaching approaches, resources, and institutional environments is the project undertaken by the American Sociological Association (see the chapter by Mauksch). Faculty can exert a significant force through participation in consortia, where the collective efforts of several colleges can be carried out better than a single institutional program. In many consortia, there are faculty committees to plan, develop, and oversee activities to carry out the intended theme. For example, sponsoring an off-campus experiential program allowing students to apply learning in nonclassroom settings and urban semesters has brought the reality of societal problems to many small-town students who, while pursuing programs under the idealist intent, gain much more in the actual outcome than campus-based learning would afford them.

Final Observations

To prevent further erosion of status, we urge faculty to reassess themselves as professionals and clearly define their role. Working from the feature distinguishing the faculty role—namely, the ability to advise on the goals and outcomes of learning—faculty can assume vigorous leadership. There are several aspects to the process.

Faculty need to think analytically about what present curricula accomplish, what methodologies work best for what purposes, and what importance student life outside the classroom has to the totality of education. Developing new curricular thrusts should be an ongoing faculty activity in response to societal needs and changes. Equally important is raising questions about basic educational assumptions and traditional purposes of acquiring knowledge. Furthermore, mutually developed objectives that address the moral, intellectual, and developmental life of students will help faculty provide vitality and teaching excellence.

In the co-curricular area there are also a variety of ways faculty can help make efficient and progressive educational decisions that will help in overcoming various external pressures. They can actively contribute to the design of career-related studies (such as internships) within disciplines, sponsor programs that have intellectual and cultural values, serve on student committees and special interest activities. This area of noncognitive education is fertile for faculty involvement and should include considerations of the many types of outcomes students seek.

Overall, it seems possible, in the turbulent times of today, that, despite many traditions, the essentially self-monitoring body of individuals called faculty may not maintain its current professional status if the participants in this role do not collectively take hold. The place to start is in the area of greatest legitimacy, the one holding the greatest potential for success: the clarification of student learning outcomes.

References

Axelrod, J., Freedman, M. B., Hatch, W. R., Katz, J., and Sanford, N. *Search for Relevance: The Campus in Crisis.* San Francisco: Jossey-Bass, 1969.

Barry, R. M. "Clarifying Objectives." In O. Milton and Associates (Eds.), *On College Teaching: A Guide to Contemporary Practices.* San Francisco: Jossey-Bass, 1978.

Bloom, B. S., Engelhart, M. D., Furst, E. J., Hill, W. H., and Krathwohl, D. R. *A Taxonomy of Educational Objectives: Handbook I: Cognitive Domain.* New York: McGraw-Hill, 1956.

Bolman, F. de W. "Not in Our Stars." In C. C. Walton, and F. de W., Bolman (Eds.), *Disorders in Higher Education.* Englewood Cliffs, N.J.: Prentice-Hall, 1979.

Bradley, A. P., Jr. *The BPS: A New Degree Alternative.* Saratoga Springs, N.Y.: Empire State College, 1974.

Bradley A. P., Jr. "Faculty Roles in Contract Learning." In D. Vermilye (Ed.), *Current Issues in Higher Education: Learner-Centered Reform.* San Francisco: Jossey-Bass, 1975.

Bradley, A. P., Jr. *The New Professional: A Report on Faculty in Individualized Education.* Saratoga Springs, N.Y.: Empire State College, Center for Individualized Education, 1978.

Brown, D. G. *The Mobile Professor.* Washington, D.C.: American Council on Education, 1966.

Brubacher, J. S., and Rudy, W. *Higher Education in Transition: An American History, 1636–1956.* New York: Harper & Row, 1958.

Caplow, T., and McGee, R. J. *The Academic Marketplace.* New York: Doubleday, 1958.

Carnegie Commission on Higher Education. *Less Time, More Options: Education Beyond the High School.* New York: McGraw-Hill, 1971.

Chickering, A. W. *Education and Identity.* San Francisco: Jossey-Bass, 1969.

Dewey, J. "President Hutchins' Proposals to Remake Higher Education." *Social Frontier,* 1937, *3,* 103–104.

Dewey, J. *Experience and Education.* New York: Collier, 1938.

Dressel, P. L., Johnson, F. C., and Marcis, P. M. *The Confidence Crisis.* San Francisco: Jossey-Bass, 1971.

Drucker, P. F. *Managing in Turbulent Times.* New York: Harper & Row, 1980.

Edwards, A. H. "Marginality and Part-Time Faculty/Mentors in Individualized Postsecondary Education Institutions." Unpublished doctoral dissertation, Walden University, 1978.

Gaff, J. J. *Faculty Self-Renewal.* San Francisco: Jossey-Bass, 1975.

Harvard University. *General Education in a Free Society.* Cambridge, Mass.: Harvard University, 1945.

Harvard University. *Report on General Education.* Cambridge, Mass.: Harvard University, 1978.

Hazen Foundation. *The Student in Higher Education: Report of the Committee on the Student in Higher Education.* New Haven, Conn.: Hazen Foundation, 1968.

Hutchins, R. M. *The Higher Learning in America.* New Haven, Conn.: Yale University Press, 1936.

Jacob, P. *Changing Values in College.* New York: Harper & Row, 1957.

Katz, J., and Associates. *No Time for Youth: Growth and Constraint in College Students.* San Francisco: Jossey-Bass, 1968.

Keeton, M. T., and Tate, P. J. "Editor's Notes: The Boom in Experiential Learning." In M. T. Keeton and P. J. Tate (Eds.), *New Directions for Experiential Learning: Learning by Experience—What, Why, How,* no 1. San Francisco: Jossey-Bass, 1978.

Kerr, C. *The Uses of the University.* New York: Harper & Row, 1966.

Ladd, E. C., and Lipset, S. M. *The Divided Academy: Professors and Politics.* New York: McGraw-Hill, 1975.

Mager, R. F. *Preparing Instructional Objectives.* Palo Alto, Calif.: Fearon Publications, 1962.

Millett, J. D. (Ed.). *New Directions for Higher Education: Managing Turbulence and Change,* no. 19. San Francisco: Jossey-Bass, 1977.

Milton, O., and Associates. *On College Teaching: A Guide to Contemporary Practices.* San Francisco: Jossey-Bass, 1978.

Moore, W. E. *The Professions: Roles and Rules.* New York: Russell Sage Foundation, 1970.

Newman, J. H. *The Idea of a University.* New York: Longman's, Green, 1947.

Ralph, N., and Freedman, M. B. "Innovative Colleges: Challenge to Faculty Development." In M. B. Freedman (Ed.), *New Directions for Higher Education: Facilitating Faculty Development,* no. 1. San Francisco: Jossey-Bass, 1973.

Rudolph, F. *The American College and University: A History.* New York: Vintage Books, 1962.

Sanford, N. (Ed.). *The American College: A Psychological and Social Interpretation of Higher Learning.* New York: Wiley, 1962.

Sanford, N. *Where Colleges Fail: A Study of the Student as a Person.* San Francisco: Jossey-Bass, 1967.

Shoben, E. J., Jr. "Student and Civil Disobedience." *Journal of General Education,* October 1968, pp. 212–229.

Stark, J. S., Terenzini, P. T., and Trani, E. "New Directions for the Student Consumer Movement." In *Current Issues in Higher Education.* Washington, D.C.: American Association for Higher Education, 1978.

Veysey, L. R. *The Emergence of the American University.* Chicago: University of Chicago Press, 1965.

Walton, C. C., and Bolman, F. deW. (Eds.). *Disorders in Higher Education.* Englewood Cliffs, N.J.: Prentice-Hall, 1979.

Wegener, C. *Liberal Education and the Modern University.* Chicago: University of Chicago Press, 1978.

Witthun, J., Kegel, M., and Haukaas, H. *After One Year: Studies of Students at Northland College.* Ashland, Wis.: Northland College, 1976.

A. Paul Bradley, Jr. has conducted research for several years on the role of faculty mentors in nontraditional education. He has served as dean of faculty of an urban comprehensive college and currently is vice president of the American Management Associates, Inc. in New York City. Bradley is a graduate of Colgate University and holds a doctorate in higher education from the University of Michigan.

Susan Olson Bolman has over twenty-five years experience in student services and has conducted several studies of student learning outcomes. She is currently a vice president at New York Institute of Technology. She is a graduate of American University and holds a doctorate from Teachers College, Columbia University.

Identifying intended outcomes can mean renewing our sense of our own disciplines as viable, dynamic modes of thinking and acting for learners at any stage. The experience of eleven institutions shows that, no matter how faculty begin, the process of clarifying outcomes has multiple effects that are worth the institutional commitment it requires.

Revitalizing the Academic Disciplines by Clarifying Outcomes

Georgine Loacker

Most of us in academe were trained within a particular discipline. Those of us who are practitioners—with teaching rather than research as a primary commitment—feel strong identification with our discipline. Most of us do most of our teaching in this discipline, and our publications tend to focus on it, not on teaching. Even those who make more general applications of their discipline in business, industry, or other professions often still identify with it.

In practicing that discipline, many college faculty members feel not unlike the bee whom Emily Dickinson describes as unconcerned about the pedigree of honey: "A clover anytime to him is aristocracy" (Dickinson, p. 1116). Most of us feel that our particular discipline, and anything a learner derives from a study of it, is "aristocracy." Therefore it is tempting to make learning outcomes, like pedigree, a consumer question. Yet, at our best, we recognize that what the discipline becomes for learners as a result of our teaching is indeed our responsibility. No doubt, then, the question—What are the learning outcomes of our degree programs?—is our concern, even if the student or the state brings it up. However, the word *outcomes* may seem limiting, tending to focus our attention upon products. Properly understood, learning outcomes involve not only products but also processes, including the developing of new attitudes. It is difficult to imagine that identifying intended outcomes could actually mean renewing our sense of our own disciplines as viable, dynamic modes of thinking and acting. *Outcomes* hardly seem like something that will enhance the intellectual excitement of life.

In order to move on more compatible semantic ground, I am therefore going to talk about the nature of the academic discipline and then come back to learning outcomes in the context of the discipline.

The Living Roots of Our Discipline

When we chose a particular discipline—even if we selected it primarily as a means to a career—most of us saw it as a way of understanding life, giving design and depth to our search for wisdom. We saw our discipline as an intellectual arena for grappling with far-reaching issues, for taking a role in revising reality and shaping the future. We saw it as a way of learning and thinking that took life from the interplay of multiple minds.

And thus it was, in its origin. Both etymology and anthropology attest to the dynamic thrust of disciplines. The very origin of the word (Latin *disciplina,* instruction, from *discere,* to learn) makes the contrast explicit: "*Discipline,* as pertaining to the disciple or scholar, is antithetical to *doctrine,* the property of the doctor or teacher; hence in the history of the words, *doctrine* is more concerned with abstract theory, and *discipline* with practice" (*Oxford English Dictionary,* 1961, p. 415). A discipline was originally an area of knowledge to be organized for serving the learner, not for possession by the learned—whether astronomy for the education of the Egyptian farmer in 3000 B.C. or philosophy for the Roman politicians in A.D. 1.

True, as educators sought to make the disciplines more accessible for learning, they managed by the same process to fragment, to isolate, and to solidify them into ends in themselves. From Aristotle's careful inventory of humankind's best knowledge of the universe, to the eventual assignment of areas of knowledge as separate administrative departments in universities, we can watch the understanding of *discipline* shift from verb to noun. In holding still these active ways of knowing and changing reality in order to examine them, we have tended to transform them into fixed objects. As learning flourished, moreover, knowledge resulted: It needed to be stored, preserved, ordered, transmitted, and added to. New generations had to acquire it. All of this encouraged a static view of each academic discipline as a definite body of knowledge, presided over by licensed guardians. Little wonder that the teaching/learning dynamic often became a matter of "covering material."

Yet, in statements of intent throughout history, we have repeated our desire to prevent our living disciplines from being reduced to lifeless objects of knowing. Our words have reiterated the necessity of connecting and reconnecting learner > thought > experience in a lively process, led by resourceful master learners. Witness as recent a document as the 1973 Carnegie Commission report, listing the "main purposes of education in the United States today, and for the prospective future" (p. 1). It begins with "the provision of opportunities for the intellectual, aesthetic, ethical, and skill development of individual students and the provision of campus environments which can constructively assist students in their more general developmental growth" (p. 1). Fourth on the list is transmission of knowledge. And Jack Embling (1974) elaborates even this idea's meaning as an active one: "It is not the mere acquisition of knowledge that matters: it is the development of intellectual curiosity, the ability to assess the value of evidence objectively and impartially, to determine realities, to distinguish what is important" (p. 18).

As faculty, we agree. And the implementation is ultimately in our hands. But how do we do it? How do we define and reaffirm those abilities that characterize a person who effectively practices our discipline in his or her life? How do we rethink the ways for connecting the learner with the lively how and why as well as the what in our field? In short, how do we rediscover and revitalize what it means to profess our discipline?

The Lifeline of Our Disciplines

In 1965, Wayne Booth, president elect of the Modern Language Association, was already gently prodding professors of English to reconsider the nature of professing and learning: "What we do not see very often are public confessions that the effort to cover more than a fraction of the indispensable subject matters has long been privately recognized by most of us as absurd. . . . It is absurd because coverage of subject matter is not in the least what we have in mind when we think of competence or distinction in our field. No one believes that what makes the difference between a man who is educated in English and one who is not is whether he knows one period rather than another" (p. 202).

What is it that we have in mind when we think of competence or distinction in our field? What characterizes someone who is educated in English or physics or social work? What does that person apply in his or her academic or nonacademic work? Once we respond to these questions, we have begun the task of specifying intended learning outcomes (or abilities or whatever we choose to call them). But then we face the real difficulty. For we realize that professing a discipline is a lifelong process, and we respect the intensity of that process. We sense that rethinking a discipline as learning will also mean rethinking how we teach it. In fact it may well mean rethinking even more, for the discipline in its fullest sense has developmental stages of its own, each to be understood in its own terms.

DISCIPLINE

PREPARE > DEVELOP > > PROFESS > > > >

We *prepare* for our life of learning as a future profess–or of a discipline by developing those abilities that enable us to think and inquire through disciplinary frameworks. Whether our career goals are academic or profess–ional in some other respect, these frameworks initiate us into the concept of disciplinary language, methodology, and conclusions. We *develop* our learning in a primary discipline by internalizing its modes of thinking and acting, by testing its frameworks, sorting its observations, and evaluating its conclusions. We *profess* a discipline once we have made its language central to our own language and its activities central to our lives, and we can extend its methods and conclusions by articulation, application, and new discovery. We profess it directly if we teach or do research in the field; we profess it directly or indirectly if we carry it into business or into a profession like medicine or social services.

These general processes took specific shape in the familiar events of our own academic lives. Whether or not the precise beginning of each stage is clear, there is some point for each of us when we began to see ourselves as no longer merely preparing but more seriously developing within a discipline. Eventually we began to see ourselves as experienced professionals.

For traditional students, the transition from preparing to developing might come as early as the choice of an undergraduate major or as late as the final months of graduate school. For adult learners, preparing and developing both may occur during years of experience in the field, while entering college and earning a degree offer a short period to consolidate those stages, fill in gaps, and begin to profess.

Graduates who profess their disciplines in academe may identify further degrees, publications, advancement in rank, and teaching awards as milestones in their professing stage. Graduates who enter nonacademic fields may find further degrees relevant, but will also identify with other milestones appropriate to their careers.

No neat boundaries divide learning into stages. The preparing, developing, and professing overlap and fuse. Yet, any individual professional who identifies with a discipline can map those stages in his or her own life.

To define *learning* or distinction in our field operationally, then, we need to focus: Learning when? When we enter Humanities I with a blank copy book, or leave the auditorium with a signed diploma, or pore over a colleague's research report? Distinction when? When we are nominees for senior honors, or for tenure, or for the Nobel prize?

At the same time, we need to understand each of the stages of a discipline in relation to all the others. We need to view them in connection with each other, as organically linked phases of a unified whole, if we would understand the discipline fully enough to participate in it. When we write a freshman examination question, or award three hours of graduate credit, or plan an agenda for a national meeting, we are either reinforcing or undermining the continuity of thinking and acting in our discipline.

Understanding each stage of a discipline in terms of the other stages means seeing each person's career in the discipline as an ongoing learning process, one that constantly changes and advances. As a learner, one needs access to that discipline at the time one is ready to enter—no matter how, when, or where. Again, at each stage, one needs access from the previous role into the new level of involvement. When American undergraduate education first began to offer majors in given disciplines, students soon sensed that becoming "disciples" would mean more than taking discrete courses. They came up sharply against their need to have the masters of the discipline make its processes accessible. In an early issue of the *Educational Review* (Overstreet, 1914), an 1899 graduate of one pioneer major program at the University of California says: "All these studies were simply separate tasks that bore no definite intrinsic relation to each other. . . . What I mean to make clear is that, although the aim which our university evidently had in prescribing work was to give us a comprehensive view before we specialized in any one subject, there was, in fact, nothing in the work that was in any true sense comprehensive at all. . . . The right studies were there; what was lacking was the conscious organization of them for the student" (pp. 169–170).

Not that we should do all the learner's organizing. But unless we make explicit what our disciplines can do, we render them inaccessible to learners. And we hinder development and transformation of the disciplines, which is ultimately our responsibility as people who profess them. True, teaching means something different at every stage of a discipline. But, at each stage, disciples need clarity and direction from master learners who see the need for demystification, lest pseudomysteries block access to the true mystery at the heart of each discipline. Identifying expected learning outcomes contributes to that clarity and direction. What we ask the newly initiated to do as an entry requirement will ultimately affect our journals and meetings, our professional lives, and whatever impact we might have on society.

Patterns of Intervention at Eleven Institutions

What actually happens when groups of faculty at institutions of higher education ask what *learning* or *distinction* or *competence* means for the undergraduate in their respective fields? Many different things occur, so many and so different, in fact, that they defy the inferring of a model. In this chapter I will look briefly at eleven different institutions where faculty have specified learning outcomes or abilities in order better to connect the learner and the learning. Along the disciplinary lifeline I have laid out, I will note the activity of each institution from its initial movement toward clarifying outcomes up to the present and analyze the patterns of impact that emerge. Finally, I will set forth some questions that need clarifying.

There are more differences than similarities among those institutions where faculty have identified intended learning outcomes and have implemented a program based on them. But by plotting their activity along the life-spectrum of the discipline, on the basis of where each faculty intervenes by clarifying expected outcomes for assessment, we can quickly highlight significant patterns.

We might begin with two institutions very different in every regard except concern for general education outcomes. At Brigham Young, a private university with 27,000 students, general education requirements since 1976 consist of specific outcomes for all students: mastery of fundamental skills (communications, basic mathematics, physical fitness and health, citizenship education); furthering of intellectual and related capabilities through the medium of subject material in substantive areas (arts and letters, social systems, natural science); and rigorous mastery of a significant skill or operational ability to the point of application. At North Adams State, a public college in Massachusetts with 2,100 students, each of several faculty volunteers this year is using identified outcomes (communications, analysis, synthesis, quantitative thinking, and valuing) to rethink at least one course, as part of an effort to evaluate the general education program.

In effect, the generating activity or key decision at both Brigham Young and North Adams was the identification of generic outcomes for general education. At both institutions this decision immediately branched over to affect teaching, because the faculty implicitly redefined their own role when they articulated expectations for their students. At both institutions learners on the threshold of their chosen disciplines (students) and learners already professing them (faculty) have thus been engaged from the start in whatever changes come about.

Because Brigham Young has designed assessments for each of the required outcomes, the influence of outcomes also reaches back into the various courses within the general education program and even into the lives of precollegiate learners who might demonstrate that they can already do some of what the faculty requires for general education. A further line of influence impinges just after the point of the baccalaureate degree, because the BYU faculty have begun some studies of their graduates in order to relate the learning they intended, the learning they observed during college, and the learning that is still active later. Therefore, although they do not see themselves identifying learning outcomes for specific majors, BYU faculty are affecting the meaning of their disciplines from several angles.

North Adams also sees their newly begun process as a single strategy that they may very likely augment or replace with another in the future. So we cannot predict precisely where the further impacts of the process of clarifying outcomes will occur. Right now more than 20 percent of the faculty are assessing and teaching toward at least one selected component of an ability they have decided fits into one of their courses and are working in cross-disciplinary support groups. They see themselves as providing a nucleus, a base of expertise to help the entire faculty begin looking toward a more extensive evaluation of their general education program. This group clearly has the potential to expand to the entire faculty and thus to all the disciplines.

A very different approach at University College, University of Louisville, concentrates on a single group of disciplines—the social sciences. In 1978, two faculty members identified the abilities necessary for successful entry into the social sciences: *acquisition* (of existing information, of the methods for individual search in the field, of methods of knowledge application and communication), *production* (of thematic organization for focusing individual search, of methods appropriate for the conduct of an individual search, of personal methods of knowledge application and communication), and *utilization* (acquiring established methods and history of cultural implementation of the discoveries of the field and the forms in which knowledge in the field has been communicated, producing culturally useful tools and applications based on the discoveries of one's search, utilizing one's discovery in cultural projects and ongoing institutions). The faculty then committed themselves to design appropriate learning experiences. Although the resulting courses were planned as part of the institution's study skills program, they actually function also as regular general education electives.

Again, the focus on outcomes necessarily engages the teaching learner as well as the preparing learner. In addition to designing and teaching outcome-oriented courses, University College faculty have published a detailed teacher's manual for developing entry abilities for the social sciences (Blum and Spangehl, 1979). With this publication, clarifying outcomes has expanded the teacher's professional involvement in collaboration with colleagues outside the college. (The phenomenon of internal collaboration, which results from and supports clarifying outcomes, is apparent in every institution studied in this chapter.)

Another interesting single division or discipline approach is a movement within the graduate division of Northwestern University School of Music. There, faculty have identified entry abilities for each area of music, from composition to history to performance. For example, in composition, one requirement for students is to demonstrate ability to create original, well-constructed musical works in contemporary idioms for a variety of performing media, in both large and small forms, appropriately and clearly notated. In music history, one ability students must demonstrate is to know music literature for each of two major style periods. In woodwind performance, a student must, among other requirements, demonstrate performance ability in chamber music of all periods. As part of a faculty development effort, teaching assistants are designing assessments and self-study modules to help new graduate students demonstrate the required entry abilities.

We can see the effects of this effort on the spectrum of the discipline by contrasting it with the Louisville University College social studies project. Both programs begin with required outcomes for the student learner's entrance into a further stage of involvement in the discipline—at University College, with initial entrance into a major field; at Northwestern, with entrance into graduate study. Both also affect teaching learners at two points—at University College, as advanced teachers and as writers; at Northwestern, as beginning teachers and as advanced teachers.

Two public institutions, Eastern Oregon State and Delaware County Community College, show how total institutional consensus creates a multiple effect, addressing all the disciplines. By 1979, at Eastern Oregon State College (1,600 students), faculty in all fields had identified outcomes for entry into individual programs, rather than generic abilities for all. Although these outcomes are still in quantitative terms like GPA and number of hours of course work, they have mapped all of their courses developmentally and filled in the gaps so that they are ready for more specific articulation of outcomes.

At Delaware County Community College, Media, Pennsylvania (6,000 students), faculty in 1977 identified generic exit abilities that all students must demonstrate. A graduate of Delaware Community College can use the basic academic skills, has an awareness of self and relation to others, can apply the meaning of career to career choices, can pursue lifelong learning, can solve problems, can analyze impacts of arts and humanities, social and economic systems, and effects of science and technology, and finally, satisfies the competencies of his or her chosen curriculum. The primary point of impact of clarifying outcomes is at the associate of arts degree stage, which, for many adult community college students with well-developed careers, marks entry into professing their disciplines.

Since 1977, each major department has further specified outcomes of its own. For example, liberal arts majors must (among other requirements) gain, by reading widely, an understanding of the vocabulary and the major concepts in areas of the arts, literature, natural and social sciences, technology, and business. The office of Management Systems, Planning, and Research has also completed several studies of Delaware graduates at work and in later schooling that enable them to compare outcomes at different stages of the learner's disciplinary involvement. The outcome-defining process has thus also influenced the learning and teaching in each major, as well as reaching into the graduate's postdegree progress in the discipline.

Both Eastern Oregon State and Delaware County Community College began by identifying expected learning outcomes at a particular point: for Eastern Oregon at entry into major programs; for Delaware, at the AA degree. Both faculties have since looked not only at their own teaching of their disciplines but also at learning outcomes at a stage of further development in practicing the discipline—Eastern Oregon through a baccalaureate writing assessment, Delaware through questionnaires administered to graduates and their employers or instructors.

A contrasting strategy is that of two private institutions often compared in current literature on competence-based higher education—Mars Hill College in North Carolina and Our Lady of the Lake University in San Antonio. Both faculties have identified six competences as generic baccalaureate learning outcomes on the basis of areas defined by Philip Phenix in *Realms of Meaning* (1964): communications, personal awareness, values, aesthetics, science, and synoptics. Both have then implemented them throughout the curriculum, making varied learning and assessment experiences available. Thus, while the outcomes were first identified as exit requirements, some may be demonstrated earlier. The process of identifying outcomes has also affected both faculties as learners in several ways: in teaching, in research, and in disseminating new curricular insights through publishing and through consulting with colleagues at other institutions.

Faculty at both institutions see the identifying of generic learning outcomes as a powerful tool for revitalizing their sense of their disciplines, one that has deeply altered their teaching and the direction of learning for their students. At Mars Hill, where several departments have also identified expected outcomes for individual majors, some faculty use these outcomes as negotiating guidelines to assess individual knowledge and abilities developed outside the classroom.

Another set of institutions where the consideration of learning outcomes has become a means of rethinking the disciplines includes three private colleges of similar size: Alverno College in Milwaukee, Mary College in Bismarck, North Dakota, and Iowa Wesleyan. In examining their processes, we come upon a significant shift in the way change takes place. The institutions considered thus far (except perhaps Delaware County Community College, where plans for dealing with the impact of outcomes on student assessment are now being made) have focused on an approach to change that is primarily *diachronic,* happening eventually through time. As one way of improving the teaching/learning process, their faculties began to identify expected characteristics of the person who has learned.

This specification of desired outcomes has then exerted its further impact in these institutions gradually, as the process has or has not found varied related points of entry into the life of the disciplines. Before the specifying of desired outcomes finds all possible points of entry, other ways of reconsidering learning and teaching may augment or replace it. Faculty (in some cases, an entire faculty; in some cases, a small group of three or thirty) may through extended dialogue have reached early consensus on a set of outcomes; but after the initial move, the cumulative succession of impacts depends essentially on whether a chain reaction occurs or whether new, unrelated strategies catch faculty attention. At Mars Hill and Our Lady of the Lake, for example, where generic outcomes have had extensive impact on the general education curriculum, the clarification of outcomes for individual disciplines may or may not occur.

The institutions I will now consider, however, have approached change more *synchronically*. In other words, they have reached a decision and then planned various simultaneous changes to support it. Having begun with varied questions (How can we improve? How can we find out if our students are doing what we say we want them to? What is unique about the education we provide?), the entire faculty in each situation struggled through to a consensus that happened to include some form of clarifying learning outcomes. Once they had agreed to try that strategy, they probed its implications for the learner and then sought to transform the total environment of the institution in support of the learner. They made explicit the points where they could foresee that redefining outcomes might reshape and revitalize the efforts of students, faculty, and administrative staff. They worked to bring about change simultaneously at these varied points; as they did so, they found change occurring at still other points. These faculties have also worked to integrate the different expressions of outcome-generated change into a synthesis, to reinforce learning from all aspects. Very early, therefore, they each articulated their developing theoretical frameworks.

Placing the processes of these three different institutions on the discipline spectrum, in order of the respective ages of each program, shows how the simultaneity of effect occurs and expands.

Since 1978, Iowa Wesleyan faculty, in working on identifying intended outcomes, have agreed on four: communications, reasoning, valuing, and social effectiveness. They have related these outcomes to the young adult development model of Douglas Heath (1977) and integrated them into a multidimensional pedagogic framework of their own. They have gradually worked to achieve consensus throughout the institution on commitment to a new model of liberal learning, one that would involve "reorganizing institutional structures for teaching effectiveness" (Iowa Wesleyan Faculty, 1978, p. 9).

Iowa Wesleyan faculty have explicitly set processes into motion "to implement and evaluate the new model of learning on a permanent basis" (Iowa Wesleyan Faculty, 1979, p. i). Therefore, though the initial defining of outcomes impacted at the graduation point, other lines of influence immediately extended to several points along the discipline spectrum. In 1979, Iowa Wesleyan began a study of seniors and freshmen on the basis of competency measures. In their Center for Participatory Learning, which opened in September 1980, they have implemented the phase of their plan that aims to provide "structured assistance to the faculty in rethinking courses and teaching strategies in the light of a goal-oriented model" (Iowa Wesleyan Faculty, 1978, p. 7). Their plan for the next five years also includes objectives that touch recruitment, retention, and dissemination. Defining outcomes will then have a widespread impact on the life of the disciplines, at points that are anticipated in a college-wide plan.

In 1976, Mary College first published intended outcomes for its graduates: communications, interaction with environment, critical thinking, valuing and Christian attitudes, aesthetic judgment, and professional development. Since then, the faculty have gradually worked out a new design for every major program that specifies outcomes in terms of academic preparation, performance skills, and professional values. For example, the science major must be able to think critically, independently, and constructively, using the scientific method to integrate, into his or her professional and everyday life, the scientific discipline (the vocabulary of science, knowledge of matter and energy in biological, mathematical, and physical systems, and their interrelationship). The faculty have also mapped all of the courses in their majors in relation to these outcomes.

In the fall semester of 1980–1981, each Mary College faculty member piloted a strategy for assessing student development in one selected class. Working together systematically in six self-selected interdisciplinary groups, faculty and administrators continue to work out cumulative strategies for learning and assessment based on these pilot programs. In only five years, Mary College faculty have redefined learning and teaching in both major areas and general education. They have also extended their professional roles into the interdisciplinary design of techniques for student assessment and program evaluation.

In the nine years since their initial specification of outcomes, Alverno College has had four classes of graduates who have demonstrated to the faculty's satisfaction those competences required for graduation: communications, analysis, problem solving, valuing, social interaction, relating to the environment, relating to the contemporary world, and aesthetic response. These have been expanded to include specialized requirements for majors and support areas as well as general education outcomes. For example, a psychology major must demonstrate eight abilities, one of which is to analyze human behavior within theoretical frameworks supported by empirical data; an English major must demonstrate eleven, one of which is to make critical judgments about written works. Alverno faculty have rethought—and continue to rethink—all of their courses to assist students in developing identified abilities. With faculty-designed instruments, faculty assess student learning at progressive stages of development, including the preentry level in communication areas.

Besides sharing what they have learned with the broader educational community through workshops and consulting contracts, the Alverno faculty hold regular visitation days and annual week-long workshops. They have published several documents describing the theoretical framework they have developed and its developing extension into specific disciplines (Alverno College Faculty, 1976, 1979; Alverno College Nursing Faculty, 1979; Earley, Mentkowski, and Schafer, 1980; Doherty, Mentkowski, and Conrad, 1979).

At Alverno, redefining learning in terms of outcomes has in turn prompted the redefining of the activity of learners in each discipline at every stage where the college is involved. Such redefinitions have strongly influenced areas where colleges have seldom heretofore been directly engaged, such as follow-up studies of graduates and faculty-designed studies of competent nonacademic professionals.

Implications for Institutions

At the heart of curricular change at Iowa Wesleyan, Mary College, and Alverno is the way their faculties use the process of identifying outcomes. For them it is an organizing principle; specifying outcomes was the initial step in developing a coherent theory by which they reshape their practice and into which they continually synthesize their experience. For most of the other institutions considered here, it is a single strategy with linear effects that may be intermittent and eventual, each dependent on its own individual power of transformation.

Synchronic/Diachronic Change. No doubt synchronic change may be more apt to occur in a smaller institution, where a more focused mission is possible and where individual faculty feel directly responsible for change and have more sense of the total institution. The spread of the larger university encourages organization by diversity, relying on that spontaneous change in various individual units that characterizes the diachronic approach. Both approaches to change seem also to be a matter of style as well as size, however. Planning is by nature diachronic, reaching from the present into the future, but institutions with a synchronic approach focus more on the intentional as their key mode of action, while those with a diachronic approach focus more on the spontaneous. And of course both approaches, the intentional and the spontaneous, interact. The faculty taking a synchronic approach plans a network of intentional actions so that when the spontaneous occurs it is not lost but is instead immediately enhanced. The faculty that takes a diachronic approach lets each spontaneous action take its own course and plans for as much development as it can sustain.

There are trade-offs to keep in mind, too. The institution moving synchronically needs to work to maintain openness and flexibility. The institution moving diachronically needs to work to establish continuity and substance. Faculty and administrators who are aware of the trade-offs can collaborate to prevent or temper them.

Interaction Among Disciplines. Another interesting phenomenon results from articulating learning outcomes. The process usually stirs up some new currents in the slow waters that stream back and forth between the separate disciplines. As faculty identify their disciplines' varied modes of thinking and acting, they discover similarities and congruities as well as distinctions. This almost inevitably turns into some kind of interaction, usually neither simple in nature nor single in direction.

At all eleven institutions studied, the generic nature of the outcomes faculty have identified shows them finding commonalities that operate in the varied settings of the disciplines and yet transcend them. Even at Eastern Oregon, while the process began with identifying entry requirements for each major, the faculty has begun looking toward generic requirements by setting a single writing competence. At several institutions cross-disciplinary structures further the interaction—competence committees that began as study groups at Mary College, organized support groups at North Adams, competence divisions at Alverno. Although Mars Hill and Our Lady of the Lake opted to associate their required abilities with specific disciplines rather than make them multidisciplinary, some combining of related disciplines still occurred—for example, math and English on the communications team; art, drama, and music on the aesthetics team.

One might expect a focus on generic abilities more often when entire faculties look at liberal education or general education outcomes. However, even in the two institutions in this study where outcomes were clarified for a single area, the outcomes tend to be generic. The competencies of academic inquiry can be viewed as occurring within three broad procedural domains at University College, University of Louisville: knowledge acquisition, knowledge production, and knowledge utilization. The acquisition of knowledge in the social sciences, humanities, or natural sciences includes procedures that are common to each of these major divisions of human knowledge (Blum and Spangehl, 1979). In the graduate division of the Northwestern School of Music, a sample competency for the performance major with specialty in harpsichord requires that the student demonstrate research skills and the ability to express ideas well both orally and in writing (*Graduate Study in Music 1979–80 . . .*, p. 10).

At Louisville, Blum and Spangehl see the phenomenon of generic outcomes as a natural result of the strong cross-disciplinary emphasis that has always been implicit in the traditional liberal arts. Their own college, in fact, has neither departments nor divisions. They also see that "process outcomes like acquiring, producing, and utilizing knowledge are free of cultural reference. They can therefore be a strong initial means of giving minority and ethnic students equal access to the heritage of liberal education—a heritage which, in traditional curricula, someone else clearly owns" (personal communication, September 1980).

Jack Pernecky, associate dean of music at Northwestern, also described what he sees happening to the discipline of music when we try to concretely imagine someone learning it:

> One can see what problem solving has to do with making music when one teaches a child. For example, when a violin teacher has modeled and explained the steps in holding a bow and the child reconstructs the hold, the question is: Has the child really learned the process or merely copied from the demonstration? The average teacher will see the model reproduced and will tell the student to go home and practice. The effective teacher will seek to develop the analytical thinking of the child, asking the young violinist to reconstruct the entire procedure by explaining and illustrating this complex action. Perhaps the child can turn around and teach the attending mother. The teacher assesses the child's approach and modifies it until the learning process is complete and accurate. The child now can tell and show the world the correct approach with confidence.
>
> The teaching/learning process is complete. With each technique taught in the same manner, the child grows—by explaining, demonstrating, integrating, and reasoning. The student becomes outcome oriented, strategy seeking, and analytical in the art of music making, (personal communication, October 1980).

Further signs of integrating the disciplines into new configurations seem evident at various institutions. At North Adams, faculty have formed a new interdisciplinary department. Our Lady of the Lake has created new integrated humanities, aesthetics, and human ecology electives. Brigham Young has designed and implemented an eight-hour honors consortium in which students select a single topic to integrate three disciplines. The eight-year cross-disciplinary dialectic at Alverno has resulted in a series of integrated science and humanities courses, a seminar in learning theory and strategies in the general education program, and a new integrated humanities major. These courses involve faculty from different disciplines, each teaching the entire course to one section of students. At Mary College, faculty would seem to have gone in an opposite direction by deciding to eliminate existing interdisciplinary courses. Yet both institutions have reached the same conclusion: Each faculty member must in effect become interdisciplinary.

The Renaissance person who engages in such interdisciplinary professing may seem an anachronism as knowledge and technology continue to explode. But that is because we still look at each discipline as an amount of doctrine to be acquired, rather than as a complex of dynamic abilities that are frequently interdisciplinary by nature.

A Place to Begin

As we have seen, faculties working to make abilities accessible to the learner follow a variety of maps as they revitalize the lives of the disciplines in their institutions. Because they keep finding new land under their feet, they need to change their maps as they proceed. And some may even seem to go in opposite directions. The stabilizing factor is the common commitment of the learner—teacher or student—to entering a life of learning, developing it, and finally professing it within the academic, professional, or business world.

Clarifying outcomes is one way to create multiple points of entry into the learning process for varied learners at varied stages. And even that way has multiple formats. It is difficult to begin, but we each know that learning our discipline has always been difficult and mastery never comes easily. Terms like *outcomes* or even *abilities* may stand in our way, but we are always breaking through semantics to get to substance.

What might happen on each of our campuses if we committed ourselves to restoring our discipline as a vital, ongoing process for every learner, including ourselves? Imagine planning into the daily practice of our discipline the same intellectual excitement we sometimes get from it spontaneously. We can begin by raising a series of questions:

1. What characterizes our discipline as a way of thinking or knowing?
2. What are the people like who have learned our discipline? What do they do well, differently, uniquely, by virtue of being associated with our discipline? How does it affect the questions they ask? The choices they make?
3. Who are the students that we serve—their backgrounds, needs, talents, career aspirations, and so forth. How can our discipline

change their lives or contribute to their careers, no matter what field?

4. What abilities learned from our discipline transfer to other human activities?
5. How does our discipline add to human society and human development?

If we answer these questions for ourselves, I submit, we will discover a treasure that time has hidden. The next step of translating our answers into outcomes will seem natural and long overdue. We will begin to realize what we have, and can do, and what we could have, and could do further—and we will renew our ability to make it available to others.

References

Alverno College Faculty. *Liberal Learning at Alverno College.* Milwaukee: Alverno Productions, 1976.

Alverno College Faculty. *Assessment at Alverno College.* Milwaukee: Alverno Productions, 1979.

Alverno College Nursing Faculty. *Nursing Education at Alverno College.* Milwaukee: Alverno Productions, 1979.

Blum, M., and Spangehl, S. *Introduction to the Social Sciences: Teacher's Manual.* Kentucky: University College, University of Louisville, 1979.

Booth, W. "The Undergraduate Program." In J. C. Gerber (Ed.), *The College Teaching of English.* New York: Appleton-Century-Crofts, 1965.

Carnegie Commission on Higher Education. *The Purposes and Performance of Higher Education in the United States: Approaching the Year 2000.* New York: McGraw-Hill, 1973.

Dickinson, E. #1627. In T. H. Johnson (Ed.). *The Poems of Emily Dickinson, 3.* Cambridge, Mass.: The Belknap Press of Harvard University Press, 1914.

Doherty, A., Mentkowski, M., and Conrad, K. "Toward a Theory of Undergraduate Experiential Learning." In M. T. Keeton and P. J. Tate (Eds.), *New Directions for Experiential Learning: Learning by Experience—What, Why, How,* no. 1. San Francisco: Jossey-Bass, 1978.

Earley, M., Mentkowski, M., and Schafer, J. *Valuing at Alverno: The Valuing Process in Liberal Education.* Milwaukee: Alverno Productions, 1980.

Embling, J. *A Fresh Look at Higher Education.* New York: Elsevier, 1974.

Graduate Study in Music 1979–80, Northwestern University Bulletin. Evanston, Ill.: Northwestern University, 1979.

Heath, D. *Maturity and Competence.* New York: Gardner Press, 1977.

Iowa Wesleyan Faculty. *Participative Learning Proposal.* Mount Pleasant: Iowa Wesleyan College, April 1, 1978. (Mimeographed.)

Iowa Wesleyan Faculty. *Evaluation Plan for Learning Grant.* Mount Pleasant: Iowa Wesleyan College, February 13, 1979. (Mimeographed.)

Overstreet, H. A. "The American College Course by a Graduate of the University of California." *Educational Review,* 1914, *26,* 169–70.

Oxford English Dictionary. Vol. 3. Oxford, England: Oxford University Press, 1961.

Phenix, P. *Realms of Meaning.* New York: McGraw-Hill, 1964.

Georgine Loacker is chair of the Division of Communications and of the Assessment Council at Alverno College, Milwaukee, Wisconsin. As a professor of English at Alverno, she participated in the development of its outcome-oriented education and has served as consultant to liberal arts faculty in colleges and universities that have sought to identify and/or assess learning outcomes. She has served as a board member and regional manager for the Council for the Advancement of Experiential Learning (CAEL), as well as designer and presenter of CAEL workshops.

Concern for the professional performance of graduates of engineering allows knowledge, operational skills, and personal development outcomes to be identified. Several programmatic approaches in operation show the potential of an outcomes orientation.

Learning Outcomes in Engineering

Lee Harrisberger

In the broad sense, all engineering programs are outcome oriented. They all address a well-defined job skill market and are sensitive to the needs of the employers of their graduates, at least concerning the knowledge base. But in the pedagogical sense, engineering programs are not overtly outcome oriented. Few currently define program exit competencies and design specific learning/training activities to achieve them. Some among the engineering faculty may endeavor to define specific learning outcomes and devise teaching activities to achieve them in their courses, but they often face formidable resistance to translating these notions into overall degree requirements.

After all, the reluctant argue, we face almost overwhelming pressure, generated by new technological changes, to maintain and advance the content and methodology of our discipline. And somehow is it not true that each engineering faculty thinks that their goals, whether defined or undefined, already produce a level of professional maturity allowing graduates to operate with relative success? Graduate engineers are in high demand, they argue, and they do very well.

Of course, what success and doing well really mean depends on one's viewpoint and is fertile ground for heated debates among faculties as well as representatives from industry. In any case, there is now a growing concern for the overall career plan and personal development of the graduate engineer. For most industrial jobs for which engineering graduates are hired, they are overtrained in engineering method and principles, while there is evidence that they are undertrained in the "software" skills of being an engineer. The discipline of engineering as presented in school is an intensely introverted, objective, cognitive activity; but, in practice, engineering is also a social activity that deals with the interpersonal, subjective, and affective, as engineers inevitably become involved with historical, moral, legal, philosophical, economic, and aesthetic dimensions of their society.

The gap that exists between the needs of the profession and the training for them is often rationalized by the belief that students should get the "hard stuff" (that is, whatever is considered difficult to acquire by oneself) in school and leave the "soft stuff" to the care of the employer or chance. But the soft is not always as soft as it may look at first. Some very large companies employing engineers have developed remarkable training programs for their young recruits lasting months and even years at full pay, giving the lie to the notion that the necessary "software" can be learned haphazardly on one's own. If schools are serious about education, they should not avoid this issue.

Moreover, the training students receive in engineering already gives them welcome entry into a variety of other professions, and when the prerequisite "software" list for an engineering career is tallied, there is a remarkable similarity with the requisite competencies defined for any liberal arts graduate. Both focus on the attributes of a mature, self-actualized person who is capable of both self-fulfillment and dealing with others in a purposeful, effective way.

The Competencies of Engineering Practice

Engineering educators keep a close watch on the needs of the profession and the relevance of the engineering curriculum to the demands of industry. The eighty-five-year-old American Society for Engineering Education (ASEE) conducts periodic surveys of employers and employees to monitor the currency of the engineering education process. Its largest and most controversial work was the 1965 Goals Report (Hawkins, Pettit, and Walker, 1965), a comprehensive study involving all aspects of engineering training. It produced a long list of recommendations for sweeping changes that, of course, generated heated opposition. Regarding specific learning outcomes, the report noted a need for increased emphasis on analysis, synthesis, and design of systems, for more flexibility to accommodate the differing aims and talents of individual students and for preparing the engineering student for leadership roles.

In the ASEE publication *Future Directions for Engineering Education* (1975b, p. 42) the authors note that "we must move to reintroduce the art of engineering into engineering education." And in the study reported in the ASEE's *Engineering Education and a Lifetime of Learning* (1975a, pp. 23–24) the following needed competencies emerged: "the engineer's education must emphasize affective as well as cognitive skills. . . . It must be one which produces engineers able to cope with others in complex controversial situations, engineers imbued with a sense of national concern and social responsibility. . . . As one becomes mature in his professional career one must not only possess technical competence but also feel vital as an individual, be able to work with others, and be able to communicate and persuade."

Similarly, the National Society of Professional Engineers, in their *Guide for Developing Courses in Engineering Professionalism* (1976, p. 2), note that "students must be imbued with the concept that knowledge alone is not enough; it must be applied professionally to assure the health, safety and welfare of consumers and the public" (additional information in National Society of Professional Engineers Publication No. 2010, 1976).

As these excerpts indicate, "software" aspects of professional preparation are recognized as necessary by the national education, professional, and accrediting bodies of the discipline. (See published lists of abilities: Accreditation Board for Engineering and Technology, 1979; and Harrisberger and others, 1976.) However, faculty background and traditions are not in general open to this in a large way—even though most faculty members will assert in good faith that it is what they mean to do.

Among all the surveys and opinion polls and publications of learning objectives, there appears a rather universal inventory of valuable assets for professional and career success, many of which are abilities traditionally associated with the liberal arts. The inventory seems to group into nine basic areas, as summarized in Table 1. Areas I-IV are essentially cognitive in nature. These abilities are generally the degree program objectives of conventional knowledge-base curricula. Areas V-VIII are the abilities that have historically made up the hidden agenda of most degree programs. That is, although these attributes are generally recognized and desired, only a fraction of current curricula contain learning activities explicitly designed to develop them. In general, most professional schools (engineering, medicine, law, business) allocate a portion of their curricula to develop some of the abilities defined in Areas V and VIII. Little attention, however, is given to Area VII and essentially no curricular activity is devoted to Areas VI or IX.

About 80 percent of the typical engineering degree program is devoted to courses in categories I and II. It is obviously content oriented. About 10 percent is devoted to category IV (Culture) and 10 percent to category V (Design). There are essentially no courses in the curriculum that

Table 1. A Proposed Competency Inventory of a Professional Engineering Curriculum

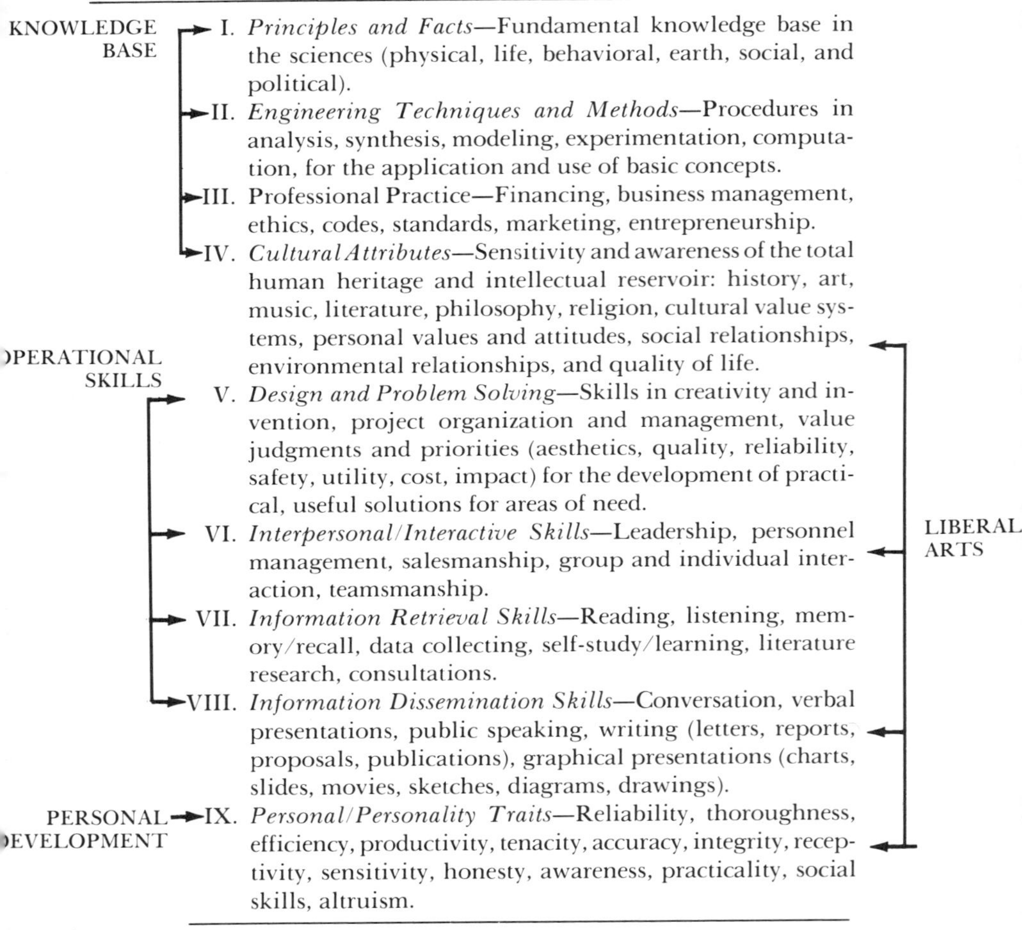

KNOWLEDGE BASE
- I. *Principles and Facts*—Fundamental knowledge base in the sciences (physical, life, behavioral, earth, social, and political).
- II. *Engineering Techniques and Methods*—Procedures in analysis, synthesis, modeling, experimentation, computation, for the application and use of basic concepts.
- III. Professional Practice—Financing, business management, ethics, codes, standards, marketing, entrepreneurship.
- IV. *Cultural Attributes*—Sensitivity and awareness of the total human heritage and intellectual reservoir: history, art, music, literature, philosophy, religion, cultural value systems, personal values and attitudes, social relationships, environmental relationships, and quality of life.

OPERATIONAL SKILLS
- V. *Design and Problem Solving*—Skills in creativity and invention, project organization and management, value judgments and priorities (aesthetics, quality, reliability, safety, utility, cost, impact) for the development of practical, useful solutions for areas of need.
- VI. *Interpersonal/Interactive Skills*—Leadership, personnel management, salesmanship, group and individual interaction, teamsmanship.
- VII. *Information Retrieval Skills*—Reading, listening, memory/recall, data collecting, self-study/learning, literature research, consultations.
- VIII. *Information Dissemination Skills*—Conversation, verbal presentations, public speaking, writing (letters, reports, proposals, publications), graphical presentations (charts, slides, movies, sketches, diagrams, drawings).

PERSONAL DEVELOPMENT
- IX. *Personal/Personality Traits*—Reliability, thoroughness, efficiency, productivity, tenacity, accuracy, integrity, receptivity, sensitivity, honesty, awareness, practicality, social skills, altruism.

LIBERAL ARTS (IV, VI, VIII, IX)

Source: Harrisberger, 1977

specifically deal with category III (Professional Practice) nor with three of the liberal arts categories—VI (Interpersonal Skills), VII (Information Retrieval), and IX (Personal Traits). A variety of activities are included to address category VIII (Communications). Some programs require a speech course and/or a technical writing course. All include almost excessive requirements for report writing in the various laboratory courses, and nearly every program requires a first year course in engineering drawing, sketching, and graphics. In addition, many senior year design programs now require oral and written presentations of the project results, which are critiqued by students, faculty, and practicing engineers.

The Educational Process in Engineering

Engineering faculty are indeed subjected to constant pressure to increase the credits required in their curricula, primarily to include new technology. Currently engineering BS programs require an average of 134 semester credit hours for graduation (with a range from 120 credits to 150), in contrast to the typical 120 required for most bachelor programs. This means an average 17 credit-hour semester load in engineering, as against the usual 15 credit-hour load.

Even though engineering programs are four-year catalog programs, it is the exceptional student who graduates so soon. The average student tenure in engineering is about 4.75 years. Part of this is due to schedule conflicts, since most curricula have rigid prerequisite schedules and few duplicate sections, especially at upper-class levels; but much is the result of workload.

The teaching/learning activity in engineering commonly follows a lecture/problem-solving format alternated with a heavy time budget for laboratories. The labs, usually about three per semester, provide extensive experience with technical phenomena. The activities cover a broad range—from training in the use of instruments and equipment to demonstration of principles and concepts to experimentation, data collecting, and design. The laboratories involve a huge expenditure of money, space, and student and faculty time. Although their objectives are essentially content oriented, the lab activities provide a rich spectrum of experiences that can contribute to the hidden agenda of ability and skill development.

Efforts have been made in some schools to begin to introduce programs more in touch with the reality of engineering practice. This has usually been done by increasing the experiential component of the program.

Over the last decade, for example, engineering educators have put increasing emphasis on the teaching of design within the curriculum. Design is broadly interpreted as the problem-solving activity associated with the practice of engineering. Historically, design activity has involved at least one senior-level course devoted to solving faculty-originated engineering problems. The problem situations, drawn from faculty experience in industry or research, focused on application of analysis, synthesis, and experimental methods. The procedures were essentially faculty supervised and the outcomes were specific and controlled.

The new design courses feature open-ended real or simulated situations found throughout industry. Attempts are made to create as realistic a problem-solving situation as possible, and there is a growing reference library of case studies developed by professors and practicing engineers. Students work in design teams (three to four people) in a client- or employer-oriented project mode. The experiences are rich in the software skills of engineering practice—covering the entire spectrum of abilities described in categories III, V, VI, VII, and VIII in Table 1.

Some schools require that seniors work directly with industry in a consultant/client mode similar to an internship. In such cases, the cooperating company pays a modest fee to cover the student team's direct expenses (phone calls, site visits, report preparation, experimentation, and so forth), while the faculty serve as project administrators in a coaching/counseling role. The faculty involvement and the awarding of credit distinguish this program from the classic cooperative education model in engineering in operation since the turn of the century. The University of Cincinnati and Drexel University, where the coop program still functions, require a fifth year of off-campus work to be negotiated by the students with employers.

Outcome-Oriented Programs in Engineering

There are also several innovative programs in engineering that have made some advances in addressing a broader array of outcomes including the liberal arts categories. They vary in how directly they define the "software" abilities they foster, from leaving them implicit in a highly experiential curriculum to spelling them out explicitly as requirements for graduation. Though all address a more realistic skill package than traditional knowledge-based curricula, none as yet has specified the abilities in terms of assessable levels of proficiency.

Harvey Mudd College and Worcester Polytechnic Institute have institution-wide programs where engineering in action is emphasized. Both schools are small private institutions that could choose to serve a specific job market and student clientele.

The Harvey Mudd College program accomplishes its goal of having graduates achieve a broad spectrum of proficiencies primarily by emphasis on the experiential component of learning (Harrisberger and others, 1976). Harvey Mudd is a relatively new (twenty-two years old) and highly selective private engineering college that has pioneered in extending the clinic-oriented format. Its entire program is focused on engineering design, without specialization in any of the traditional disciplines of engineering. This design orientation signals an emphasis on the skills of engineering practice.

At Harvey Mudd all students are required to enroll each year in the clinic program where they work on contracted (funded) projects solicited from local industries. Concurrently, they study a traditional degree program of courses offered in the same teaching style as courses in any other engineering school. One unique requirement of the Harvey Mudd degree program is that some 40 percent of the credits must be in the humanities, in contrast to the Accreditation Board for Engineering and Technology (ABET) requirement of only about 10 percent. Many engineering faculty find it incredible that the college can produce such competent graduates with such a high percentage of nonengineering courses, but it must be remembered that Harvey Mudd can attract and select the best among engineering students.

The Harvey Mudd program develops competence in problem solving, project management, research, and experimentation reporting and communicating, almost exclusively by the real life internship experiences in its clinic program. There are no prepublished outcomes or skill requirements to be met to qualify for graduation. Nor are there any competency exams organized. Students receive traditional grades in each course (including clinic), which are part of the traditional means of meeting graduation requirements.

The Worcester Polytechnic Institute (WPI) program likewise involves a full institutional commitment and is now past its tenth year (Grogan, 1979). At WPI, all the familiar procedures of traditional programs were purposely dropped to strengthen the focus on the objective of certifying qualifications. Qualification entails a week-long series of written and oral examinations before faculty juries. Students admit themselves to the program and proceed essentially by independent study. There are no grades, no required courses, although the student must show that he or she has done acceptable study in a list of required subject areas. To graduate, the student must submit two projects (similar to undergraduate theses), one in an engineering major and one in a humanities minor.

Although they are not specifically articulated as degree requirements, the WPI program focuses are development of self-learning skills, problem solving, project management, mature scholarship, sound engineering skill and judgment, research skills, and communication skills. The program easily met the accreditation requirements and has not received any criticism that its independent study approach weakens the engineering knowledge base. It has been commended for its ability to provide a broad range of experiences and training in the "software" skills of engineering practice. The program is skillfully administered by the faculty and has helped to produce an increase in enrollment and an increase in the number of exceptionally qualified students.

The certification of competency at WPI is patterned essentially on the engineering faculty's traditions in the evaluation of projects, written exams, engineering reports, and oral examinations. In courses, the faculty administer exams and quizzes that serve essentially as formative evaluations indicating to both teacher and student whether acceptable progress is being made. The program did not set out to devise or design specifically different procedures for measuring and certifying the graduation qualifications of its students, but during program development the faculty refined its efficiency and skill in assessing the large number of qualifying exams each year.

The Department of Mechanical Engineering at the University of Massachusetts has also been running a program since 1972 in professional practice-directed engineering education (Harrisberger and others, 1976). Here, as at Harvey Mudd and WPI, the emphasis is on actual industrial projects. Certain skills (for example, in learning, communication, human relations, planning, experimentation, innovation) and certain behaviors (for example, reliability, thoroughness, social concern) are explicitly encouraged, but criteria and levels are not defined formally. The key to the success of this small program rests on the system of audit whereby students receive rapid, personal, and detailed feedback on their performance so they can take corrective action if needed. The auditor, with whom the student meets individually and frequently, is not a lecturer but an incisive questioner, a friendly but open critic, and a demanding coach.

Other institutions have gone somewhat further in defining the liberal arts abilities they seek to develop in their students. The Design Clinic program for seniors in mechanical engineering at the University of Alabama, Tuscaloosa (Harrisberger, 1978, 1979a, 1979b), for instance, includes a career-readiness course that specifically addresses the spectrum of competencies of engineering practice (Areas III, V, VI, VII, VIII, and IX in Table 1). The three-credit course provides a series of diagnostic evaluations and practice in most of the interactional skills that are needed to conduct a client-oriented engineering project.

A unique feature of the career-readiness course is the emphasis on personal development (Area IX). The Myers-Briggs Personality Indicator is used to identify the basic personality profile of each student. These profiles are shared by all and used by students to assist each other in identifying their own behavior preferences as well as the styles of their colleagues. Attention focuses on the effects their own basic personality attributes have on the personal skills demanded by engineering project activity.

During the course, students also engage in a variety of learning activities drawn from the university's Schools of Management and Communication that deal with verbal presentations, small group effectiveness and leadership, conflict management, nonverbal skills development, and so forth. All activities in these "software" areas are directly related to and exercised in concurrent engineering project activity.

Following the career-readiness course, students enter the clinic activity. In the clinic, each student works as part of a three-person consultant team for an engineering client solicited from a wide range of engineering intensive companies. Certification of accomplishment is achieved by requiring each team to present their project report to a faculty jury (dress rehearsal) prior to delivering a written and verbal presentation to the client. The grade in the clinic is based on scores given by the juries.

Finally, the Cooper Union Engineering School has received funding to develop an outcome-oriented curriculum that resembles the format and competencies of some of the pioneering competency-based programs among liberal arts colleges (Huckaba, Le Mee, and Rakow, 1980; Le Mee and Rakow, 1978; Le Mee, Stecher, and Shannon, 1977). The Cooper program defines specific "software" skills according to three levels of proficiency. Eight courses have been selected for developing proficiency in three key professional competencies: problem solving, communication, and value clarification. The intent is to develop these competencies and assess them against stated criteria, within the context of traditional curriculum subject matter and methodologies. This ambitious and idealistic program is still in its initial stage, but it could well be the model for the future evolution of "software"-oriented programs in engineering.

Conclusion

The evidence clearly suggests that engineering education shares the same needs and objectives as all other programs concerned for the career capabilities of their graduates. It seems inevitable that career-oriented disciplines must, as an integral part of their programs, provide for their students' development of liberal arts abilities.

Fortunately, engineering educators have been bitten by their own bug. By nature they are motivated to implement new concepts, to refine and optimize the efficiency and effectiveness of everything they deal with. They also enjoy the advantage of a national society as a forum for improving their educational process.

We are evolving as educators toward equal concern for who we teach as well as what. And since we all teach students, we find ourselves listing the same outcome objectives as fundamental prerequisites for career success. Some of us are already attempting to define levels of proficiency and to create assessment methods for those abilities that have been generally recognized as important throughout the profession. As engineering educators, we will become increasingly involved in exploring these new methods and procedures, as we strive to improve the effectiveness of the teaching/learning processes we design.

References

Accreditation Board for Engineering and Technology. *Criteria for Accrediting Programs in Engineering in the United States.* New York: Accreditation Board for Engineering and Technology, 1979.

American Society for Engineering Education. *Engineering Education and a Lifetime of Learning.* Washington, D.C.: American Society for Engineering Education, 1975a.

American Society for Engineering Education. *Future Directions for Engineering Education.* Washington, D.C.: American Society for Engineering Education, 1975b.

Grogan, W. R. "Performance-Based Engineering Education and What It Reveals." *Engineering Education,* February 1979, pp. 402–405.

Harrisberger, L. "Creating a Professional Competency B.S. Curriculum in Engineering." In *Proceedings, Frontiers in Education Conference,* Seventh Annual Conference, University of Illinois-Urbana, October 24-26, 1977. Washington, D.C.: American Society for Engineering Education, 1977.

Harrisberger, L. "Career Readiness: A Survival Course in Mechanical Engineering." In *Proceedings, Southeast Conference on Engineering Education,* North Carolina State University, April 1-3, 1979. Washington, D.C.: American Society for Engineering Education, 1979a.

Harrisberger, L. "Developing the Compleat Engineer." *Proccedings, Frontiers in Education Conference,* Seventh Annual Conference. University of Illinois-Urbana, October 24-26, 1977. Washington, D.C.: American Society for Engineering Education, 1979b.

Harrisberger, L., Heydinger, R., Seeley, J., and Talburtt, M. *Experiential Learning in Engineering Education.* Washington, D.C.: American Society for Engineering Education, 1976.

Hawkins, G. A., Pettit, J. M., and Walker, E. A. *Goals of Engineering Education—The Preliminary Report.* Washington, D.C.: American Society for Engineering Education, 1965.

Huckaba, C., Le Mee, J., and Rakow, A. "Engineering—The Truly Liberal Education for the Future." In *Proceedings, Ninth Annual Conference, American Society for Engineering Education,* Niagara Falls, Canada, October 15-17, 1979. Washington, D.C.: American Society for Engineering Education, 1980.

Le Mee, J., and Rakow, A. "Competence Definition and Assessment Plan in a Competence-Oriented Program." In *Proceedings, Frontiers in Education Conference,* Seventh Annual Conference, University of Illinois-Urbana, October 24-26, 1977. Washington, D.C.: American Society for Engineering Education, 1978.

Le Mee, J., Stecher, M., and Shannon, T. "Liberal Professional Education: A Proposal for the Holistic Approach to the Engineering Curriculum." In *Proceedings, Frontiers in Education Conference,* Seventh Annual Conference, University of Illinois-Urbana, October 24-26, 1977. Washington, D.C.: American Society for Engineering Education, 1977.

National Society of Professional Engineers. *Guide for Developing Courses in Engineering Professionalism.* Washington, D.C.: National Society of Professional Engineers, 1976.

National Society of Professional Engineers. Publication No. 2010. Washington, D.C.: National Society of Professional Engineers, 1976.

Lee Harrisberger is currently professor of mechanical engineering at the University of Alabama. He has been an engineering educator for over thirty years, including service as a department head and dean. He has been active in educational innovation and development, directing a variety of workshops on teaching techniques for engineering faculties, and serves as consultant on educational development and is past president of the American Society for Engineering Education.

Increasing concern in art education for the student's learning needs in both cognitive and affective domains requires that attention be given to more than products developed. The creative learning process is strengthened by attention to personal as well as product outcomes.

Outcomes for the Learning Artist

Arthur Greenblatt
James Striby

The real process of learning in art is obscured by several myths. One of these derives directly from the aura that surrounds the intuitive aspect of art. It perpetuates itself in the romantic image of the artist as an individual whose thinking strategies are almost wholly in the leaps and bounds category. Such an individual is most concerned with pushing the boundaries of conventional thought, goes in a variety of artistic directions while learning, is impatient with structure, and intensely pursues information that enlightens by sudden insight. There is no question that such artists exist and that they are often successful. But to draw general inferences about learning from this romantic notion of the artist is to cut off entry for most potential learners of art.

This image of the artist, supported by the fact that many successful artists have never had formal art training, gives recurring birth to the notion that all an individual really needs to become an artist is talent. It tends to overlook the fact that accountants have a talent for math and chemists a talent for science. It cuts off the development of talent by denying the need for consciously developing it.

Most art educators have long abandoned the myth of the artist as popular and unsophisticated. They recognize that what distinguishes the adult learner, in art as in every other field of learning, is the ability to achieve conceptual organization and synthesis. It is the adult learner who is increasingly able, from adolescence onward, to infuse self-expression into a structure of ideas and to marshall skills into the organic execution of a design. The mature artist is a person who structures his or her emotion, thought, and action, whether by a carefully thought out plan or by a more intuitively guided pattern of discovery. Art is not easily learned or quickly mastered—not because it is a romantic mystery but because it is such a conceptually and experientially sophisticated process.

Another myth, however, frequently blocks the art educator's vision of how to assist learning artists to develop abilities and to evaluate their development—the myth that focuses on product as the sole sign of accomplishment. Visual arts education has been traditionally affected by public emphasis on product. Products—paintings, sculptures, prints—are critiqued, graded, sold, displayed, hidden, destroyed, given away, or cherished. They reflect an individual's taste, skill, knowledge, culture, level of expertise and emotions, as well as peer and teacher input and direction. They are certainly outcomes of the learning experience.

Once removed from the learning environment, of course, art works can be judged by a different set of standards unrelated to the learning process. This judgment may be valid in the new setting, but it can confuse the learner. Even for the accomplished artist, the product may be an end of sorts during its creation, yet it is also always part of the artist's ongoing development and commitment. In an educational setting, the product is likewise always a means to an ongoing end. It is a record of the individual student's learning process.

Art educators who make judgments about a student's learning based simply on the existence of the product, unwittingly assume that the product adequately represents the achievement of the objectives and goals of the learning experience. The fact is that we cannot readily determine whether a completed art work evidences intended skills and understandings unless we have clear knowledge of the teacher's and learner's intentions. Though the work may be of exhibition quality, we cannot evaluate it as a product of learning without knowledge of the learning experiences that have led to it.

Art as Developmental Learning

Learning in art is not a haphazard process and should not be treated as such. At all levels of visual art education, there are attitudes and values to be developed, skills and concepts to be learned and used. The studies and writings of Lowenfeld and Brittain (1970), which trace developmental stages in self-expression through art, provide a rather clearly defined statement of what can be expected in the average person's growth from approximately age two through twelve. The individual's development can be reinforced during these stages by formal education, as long as the learning environment and types of art activities are appropriate to the specific age levels.

At about age thirteen, it first becomes possible for intellectual concerns about art to enter the individual's consciousness. This is the starting point for training the mature artist. Of course, some artists actually start at a later age; but adult art education begins with psychomotor, affective, and cognitive learnings that focus on the same basic concerns whether the student is thirteen, thirty, or sixty. In fact, the abstract learning abilities that emerge at this stage are so central that, while a good elementary art program will benefit all who experience it, any adult learner may begin and successfully pursue art studies without previous training.

The work of Benjamin S. Bloom and his colleagues has provided educators with a significant and useful stimulus to help us perceive the patterns of development in the adult learner. Bloom's (1956; 1971; Krathwohl and others, 1956) taxonomies in the cognitive and affective domains are particularly valuable in this regard. It is indeed unfortunate that Bloom and his colleagues declined the challenge of thinking through a similar sequence in the psychomotor domain, an area in which art educators have more interest and experience than most of their colleagues in higher education.

While complex in content and implication, Bloom's taxonomies may be simplified to the point of regular usage in the learning and teaching of art, just as Munsell's complex color system is so often simplified to a basic color wheel.

Affective Domain

The affective domain provides opportunities to address the learner at his or her point of readiness in developing emotional involvement and commitment to the study of art as a serious pursuit. Too little attention has been paid to the fact that people learn when they are ready to learn. If we can determine the general level of a student's readiness for involvement, we can more effectively encourage further development. Since involvement varies according to the individual, we can permit students to progress through the affective learning process at different speeds, just as they do through cognitive and psychomotor growth. Bloom's taxonomy in the affective domain (Krathwohl and others, 1964) can provide helpful insights here, as it outlines a continuum from simple awareness to a possible life outlook.

Receiving. This level involves simple awareness that an object or subject exists. The aware learner may then reject the subject or accept it, later possibly giving it actual attention and interest. We have all met with this as it appears in the beginning student who simply identifies art as including a limited range of media—drawing, painting, perhaps sculpture. Most art educators work constantly to develop students' awareness at this level, to include not only the wide array of media in the fine arts and crafts but also the daily omnipresence of art in architecture, environmental design, product and industrial design, the communications media, and so on.

We can also observe this stage in relation to the subjects of art. Here, introductory design and studio courses do not simply develop the student artist's psychomotor skills and extend his or her range of techniques. They also steadily sharpen the student's ability to focus perception intensely and seriously on a variety of representational subjects and nonrepresentational concepts or problems, learning to see them as fit subjects of art.

Responding. This stage involves not just willingness to attend but active attention. The learner is doing something beyond merely perceiving. Initially, the learner responds out of obligations to an instructor's demands, directions, or encouragement. Eventually, if the learner's accumulated experience is successful, it enables him or her to discover and respond with further interest.

We see this in the beginning art student who speaks about his or her own response to particular museum art works but only because a teacher asked. Several museum trips later, he or she goes back to a particular exhibit independently. Similarly, in a studio course, a student may dutifully charcoal one still life subject after another and then one day discover and become fascinated by the play of light on glass, taking off on an intense, private quest. Art educators have all seen this occur; in fact, they probably teach for it, though not by coherent design.

Valuing. Here the learner personally engages with the subject, internalizing it and showing sustained interest. From an initial care and exploration, to a willingness to be identified with the subject, and then to commitment to it, the learner comes to value the subject openly on nonrational grounds.

We have all seen a student spend months as the willing acolyte of a particular faculty master or argue intractably in almost every discussion for a particular school or style. We have seen another suddenly ignite with excitement about a particular medium, spending every free hour at the studio and turning in a dozen aquatints when three are required. And the same spark can be struck from subject matter, as when a novice sculptor is willing to sacrifice speedy progress toward a degree in order to explore the complexities of modeling the human figure for an extra semester.

Art curricula seldom directly address the student's development at this level. But it is a crucial turning point—for it is this ability for active, self-sustaining involvement that makes becoming an artist a real possibility.

Organizing. Here the learner feels the need to relate values coherently, having become involved with several subjects and having attached feelings directly to them. Here he or she begins to develop a personal philosophy, integrating intellect, background, experiences, and tastes into some kind of system.

This stage, all too often left to informal hallway conversations and late night "bull sessions," marks the developing artist's ownership of his or her field. Here the philosopher/historian in each artist sketches a view of what art means in human life and where it has taken significant shape, framed and annotated by personal value judgments and commitments. Here the studio artist brings together experiences in several media to form a serious critical estimate of where he or she can work most effectively and what each medium can uniquely enable him or her to say. Here, too, are the first attempts to understand one's preferences for certain subjects and elements, certain challenges, as coming out of one's sense of meaning.

Characterizing. The individual is now characterized by the subject. It is a defining part of his or her life. The learner is knowledgeable and confident, able to make judgments, ready to revise judgments in the light of new evidence, and has so completely internalized the subject that he or she cannot be separated from it.

This is where the developing artist makes a more precise commitment to specialization over a significant period. The painter commits two years to large canvas studies of natural light in artificial spaces; the ceramicist joins a cooperative studio in Tennessee or moves to Japan to learn classical porcelain techniques; the graphic designer invests the early years of his or her career with a small advertising firm. Maturing as person and artist, the committed professional experiments, alters, and expands personal style through long-term commitment. Experiencing and expressing become increasingly integrated, as do medium and subject matter, artist and art.

The complexity of all that goes on in the affective realm suggests many aspects of art ability that cannot be seen in the product alone. Examining an art work, we can evaluate some of the affective outcomes relating to the artist's attitude toward his or her subject. And these judgments are by inference only, even with an accomplished artist. In order to make attitudes toward different media and toward art itself available for judgment, we must look to the artist's association with art beyond the product. Obviously one cannot follow the individual around. But we can look for his or her articulating of attitudes and values in activities like presentations, reflections on periods of development and changes in attitude, mounting a show, and writing analytic program notes for individual works.

Thus, the affective domain provides an important framework for art learning. Not only does it take into account the feeling and emotion that figure to a large extent in the creative process; it also challenges art educators to consider how to assist each developing artist to move through a complex pattern of deepening identification with and commitment to art itself, to a particular professional role or roles, and to a succession of styles, points of view, and expressions of felt meaning.

Cognitive Domain

Although every artist continually changes and grows in the affective and psychomotor abilities so prominent in the practice of art, cognitive ability plays a unique and central role in adult art learning. Regardless of style, media, or professional direction, the artist consistently performs the one essential activity common to all artists—solving a problem. Each new sheet of paper, blank canvas, hunk of clay, or bolt of yarn represents a new problem seeking a unique solution. The making of art is an intellectual pursuit in every sense of the word.

As the learner in art moves from simple skill exercises to putting something together with the materials, design principles come into play. In Bloom's (1956) cognitive taxonomy, the early stages of development deal with knowledge and comprehension. (The taxonomy within the cognitive domain has six levels: knowledge, comprehension, application, analysis, synthesis, evaluation.) Principles are taught in line, form, color, texture, visual balance, and so forth, which are appropriate to the general knowledge and skill of the learner. With painting, the learner may practice mechanical skills while dealing with a specific problem involving a color principle such as color mixing, complementaries, value tones, and so forth. Interest in solving such a problem provides motivation for further skill development as well as for learning concept principles.

As the student of art learns principles in relation to skills, he or she will be able to engage in problems and exercises that show understanding of what has been learned. In a sequential development, the learner must relate learned facts and principles to subsequent activities that build principle upon principle with continuous skill practice. The wise learner will look to knowledge gained from previous problems to apply in new situations. By recognizing this process, he or she will develop conceptual learning because the art activities function as a means to that end rather than an end in themselves.

As the learning process continues, the emphasis for the student will shift from the acquisition of knowledge and skill to a higher level of comprehension in which application becomes an emphasis. The learner puts information together to solve more generalized problems. Thus, a still life setup that may have been used at an earlier stage to teach the juxtaposition of shapes or colors becomes a general problem in which the student incorporates accumulated knowledge and applies it to the problem as a whole.

At this level of development, it will be important for the student to analyze the problem. Whenever confronting a general problem, the problem solver must be able to determine a starting point. The ability to do so presupposes a considerable amount of groundwork. When the learner has reached the analysis level, the rush to synthesis truly begins. The striving for the art product continually motivates the learner to acquire new knowledge and skills, better understandings, and relationships to apply.

Given this higher level of sophistication, the learner is able to make judgments and decisions based upon clearly understood criteria. If the problem is a landscape painting, the individual will be able to select a scene that represents an appropriate mood, select and reject parts of that scene, design a composition of interest, select colors based upon their psychological effect, and so forth. Judgments regarding appropriate media and technique, relationships to style, and an individualistic approach are at the individual's command. Thus, emphasis must move from what to how-to to why. Real emphasis on aesthetics cannot occur until a practical base has been structured.

It is important to remember that this intellectual development in the broad curricular sense is based upon the emphasis of certain kinds of activities within a developmental stage. In a single learning experience or in a long-range series, several levels of the taxonomy may be operative. Each new bit of information should help add to the student's comprehension. Principles should be applied and analyzed within the framework of the activity. In art, a product (even in the form of a simple exercise) is almost always a result of the activity. Judgments must be made on a continuous basis, in order for the students to gain experience in decision making. Aesthetics are always important. But if the student is faced with solving problems based in synthesis or evaluation objectives before he or she is ready, the frustration level will be very high.

Many of the problems learners face can be understood as disoriented taxonomy. Sequence is often missing from an education plan. Far too often students are asked to make evaluative judgments with insufficient background, leaving the beginner with an inner sense of having to defend likes and dislikes. Most disciplines rely heavily upon professional judgment. You hardly ever hear anyone say, "I don't know anything about psychology, but I know what I like!" Yet it is not at all uncommon for a beginner in art to be called upon to make profound judgments.

At the same time, much learning in art, as in other fields, ends at the knowledge level. Even though this is the lowest level in the cognitive domain, the simple passing on of knowledge can often be the sum total of an entire study. Obviously, there is much to be gained from educational planning based on a developmental understanding of cognitive learning. The adult learner, armed with no more than a general knowledge of Bloom's (1956) cognitive domain, can better understand his or her own learning level and develop realistic learning strategies. The teacher can better identify expected learning outcomes and thus construct a curriculum of sequential learning experiences and design appropriate assessments.

Many cognitive abilities can be shown, and thus assessed, in the work itself. We might, for example, be looking for a learner's ability to use analogous colors or create a mood with color by psychological affects. We can evaluate either of these in the work itself, which reveals the degree to which the artist understands the nature of various colors as well as elements like the effects of their placement or intensity.

When we as art educators can apply a general understanding of Bloom's domains—both cognitive and affective—to create a developmentally structured educational process, learning in art can take place in a manner that attends to both the intellectual and aesthetic concerns of teachers and students. Continuing to state vague objectives or staying within the lower levels of knowledge and awareness are not necessary in order to retain the so-called romantic mystery of artistic expression. In art education, we can create systematic structures that provide for both cognitive and affective learning, as well as sophistication in process skills. The approach is simply to place the emphasis on what the student will be able to do. In art, adapting objectives to the cognitive and affective taxonomy is easy, since the student can demonstrate every level in concrete learning activities. To interpret knowledge and affective experience and translate them into visual form, the art student must inevitably learn to remember, identify, describe visually, receive, and respond. The artist applies conceptual knowledge and skills, as a problem solver, constantly analyzing his or her knowledge to determine how to apply it to the problem and, at the same time, developing values and attitudes that will characterize him or her as an artist. Synthesis is virtually imperative, as is developing a personal philosophy, since solutions to art problems require tangible products. Nor can the artist escape the demands of judgment and evaluation, applying it to each of his or her own efforts as a lifelong discipline that he or she identifies with and takes responsibility for shaping.

Art as Creative Learning

How do the affective and cognitive come together in the student's learning? Clearly, they intermingle in individual situations. Each student changes at different rates in different areas, with different individual styles and interest in different media. Thus, each learning experience has its own peculiar blend of affective, cognitive, and psychomotor. Yet, current systems of art education almost exclusively employ conventional teaching strategies, despite diverse operating strategies that do seem to emerge among art students.

In the execution of a single work, we can see elements integrating differently into the strategies of individual students. One student may envision the end product, working out well in advance the details of the form that product will take. He or she may, for example, thoroughly plan a painting in regard to size, subject, and composition. In the planning stage, the student may make detailed sketches and deal with all creative aspects. Once the final process of execution is under way, the mechanical skills of the student take over completely, since the actual creative work has been accomplished. Such students are highly concerned with the end product and tend to develop emotional attachments to the completed work.

Another student may begin working in a given medium and develop the end product more spontaneously as he or she goes along. In painting, the student may begin the application of paint to the surface with only a vague concept of the end result. The composition develops in the process, and the creative aspects emerge throughout the completion of the work. By the time one work is completed, the student may be anxious to start another; several works may be even in progress at once. We can find this approach in students who are much more interested in process than product. For them, art is doing, and while the end product is pleasing and rewarding, they show less emotional attachment to it.

A third major strategy is a combination of these but is a consistent pattern within itself. The student may have a vaguely definite end product goal. If it is a painting, the student may envision a product of a specific nature: depicting a scene, conveying a mood, or perhaps concentrating on a style. The student then begins to paint, perhaps after having sketched a compositional outline on the surface. As the painting develops, it may go several ways within the preestablished boundaries, so that any one of several possibilities in the end product is a satisfactory conclusion. Emotional attachments to the end product will vary, often depending on the degree to which the student is satisfied with the end product.

Most professional artists will be able to place themselves on a spectrum between these three categories. For the artist who does not teach, such information is usually curious and interesting. For the teacher of art, it is vital. Teachers, especially at the college level, too easily tend to teach in exactly the same manner in which they themselves learn. But, in designing a single learning experience, a course, or a curriculum, we are, in effect, trying to build a matrix in which the student seeking to develop art ability can find the means to combine individual style and strategy with the developmental stage he or she might be in. As a discipline, art naturally lends itself to this.

No matter what the media, the apprentice artist gradually develops a series of skills and attitudes that enable him or her to give increasingly sophisticated expression to emotional experience. These are based on a hierarchical structure inherent in art that seems obvious to articulate but is astoundingly absent from teaching. Faculty need to make that structure explicit in order to determine which principles students should learn in order to develop levels of understanding appropriate to their age and experience level.

The major concept of design, for example, along with its related subconcepts (such as composition, balance, structure, surface elaboration) forms the foundation of experiences in early art education. The learner who has progressed through basic design studies will most likely be ready to apply that concept and others in various areas of studio art like painting, ceramics, or printmaking. The level of sophistication of that learner's understanding will depend on how many principles and process steps he or she has learned (and how well) in constructing concepts for him or herself.

Analyzing a single studio area of art sequentially also reveals what goes into structured development in the discipline of art. To successfully engage in printmaking, for example, a student must have acquired an interest and must have developed certain manipulative skills. But what the student knows and understands about printmaking will most directly determine his or her ability to perform. He or she has developed either a limited or sophisticated concept of printmaking, in relation to such specific subconcepts as silkscreen, relief, and intaglio. And each of these subconcepts in turn has at some point been developed as a concept. Thus, a concept of printmaking would be a construction of all the principles one knows about printmaking as well as all the process steps one can perform.

If a student is going to be able to demonstrate specific knowledge and skill, those things that he or she must learn in order to get there become quickly apparent. Therefore, to develop a curriculum that is based on the structure of the discipline and provides for sequential transfer of learning is to identify outcomes. The essential aspect of all outcome or performance-based education is that attention focuses on what the learner will be able to do as a result of the learning experience. The usual approach to teaching emphasizes what the teacher will do, and far more learning is assumed to have taken place than is ever actually demonstrated. Yet, paradoxically, in art far less teaching is attempted than such an emphasis implies. Outcomes that focus on what the learner will be able to do make evaluation more realistic. They delineate which elements of the performance or work are relevant and thus dispel the product-centered myth.

When attention is given to what the student is to learn in regard to concepts and skills, the teacher's freedom is also increased to a great extent. Activities, problems, and art media that may be used to teach almost any principle in art are virtually endless. The teacher can also accommodate a greater variety of students' learning strategies. Within a structure that clarifies a hierarchy of disciplinary concepts, the teacher has greater flexibility in the nature of the assignments and the manner in which the student may evidence his or her learning.

The more clearly the developmental patterns and learning strategies of art students are recognized by both students and teachers, the more teachers can provide learning experiences appropriate to the individual's natural approach to learning—and the more students can come to understand themselves. Knowing his or her own tendencies in learning also helps the learner adjust and adapt to problems that require self-discipline or developing alternate strategies. This is especially important for the adult student, since he or she must ultimately have acquired a breadth of strategies to chart his or her own course of commitment as a professional.

We must address the problems of providing a curriculum for art students that will satisfy their practical nature, retain their sense of romance, provide for differences in teaching methods and learning strategies, cope with expanded age ranges among students, take into account individual differences and goals, teach definitive skills, attend to aesthetics, provide a well-rounded education, and prepare people for productive, fulfilling careers in the profession of art.

These tasks cannot be achieved with vague language or with inherited curricula and unexamined educational goals. We must be able to foster educational progress by defining learning outcomes in a sequential curriculum, so that our products—both the students we turn out and the art works they create—will reflect the successful attainment of our intentions and hopes as educators.

References

Bloom, B. S., Engelhart, M. D., Furst, E. J., Hill, W. H., and Krathwohl, D. R. *Taxonomy of Educational Objectives.* Handbook I: *Cognitive Domain.* New York: McKay, 1956.

Bloom, B. S., Hastings, J. T., and Madaus, G. F. *Handbook on Formative and Summative Evaluation of Student Learning.* New York: McKay, 1971.

Krathwohl, D. R., Bloom, B. S., and Masia, B. B. *Taxonomy of Educational Objectives.* Handbook II: *Affective Domain.* New York: McKay, 1956.

Lowenfeld, V., and Brittain, L. W. *Creative and Mental Growth.* 5th ed. New York: Macmillan, 1970.

Arthur Greenblatt is dean of the Center for Creative Studies College of Arts, Detroit, Michigan.

James Striby is dean of faculty.and professor of art at Moore College of Arts, Philadelphia, Pennsylvania.

Both are painters who have exhibited widely and are represented in private collections throughout the United States. Both have taught art to students at all levels. While together at the Maryland Institute College of Art, they created, designed, and implemented the combined course modular structure for teacher education, a nontraditional and innovative approach and one of the first competency-based art teacher education programs developed in the United States. They have jointly devised and implemented several special art programs for nontraditional students, including art teacher training for the elderly.

Individualized education requires special attention to be given to the role of the professor-student relationship in the learning process. Two case studies highlight the issue of quality in these relationships, and suggest questions for future research.

Quality Relationships in Individualized Education

Ernest G. Palola
Marlene J. Evans

During the 1970s, many new programs in postsecondary education were developed to address the student as an individual, active learner. Students, many of whom were adults, were given opportunities to manage and adapt the learning process to fit their personal needs, selecting how, what, and when learning would occur. In response to the more participatory role taken by students, faculty enlarged their concerns to encompass one-to-one teaching/learning relationships, requiring that more attention be given to the interpersonal skills needed to deliver individualized educational services (Hall and Palola, 1981).

Individualized learning/teaching modes, perhaps more than other approaches, require attention to intended learning outcomes. Clearly defined learning outcomes are factors that can affect the content, scope, and pace of the learning process. With the student assuming more responsibility, faculty find it is important to explain how outcomes are to be achieved as well as to communicate to students what outcomes are expected.

A cursory overview of the literature on individualized education shows a number of studies that describe the background of faculty and their role in individualized programs (Berte, 1976; Bradley, 1975, 1978; Clark,

1975; Eldred and Marienau, 1979; Johnson, 1975; Medsker and others, 1975) and on student's background and role (Claxton and Ralston, 1978; Peterson and others, 1979; Vermilye, 1976; Weathersby and Tarule, 1980). This material addresses the three key components of most educational approaches, traditional or nontraditional—faculty, student, and program. Some additional studies address the learning contract as the unit of analysis to explain the individualized learning process (Berte, 1976; Lehmann, 1975, 1980; Henderson and Hyre, 1979; Wald, 1978). However, little attention has focused specifically on how to clarify and achieve intended learning outcomes, with the exception of Wald, who explored contract development.

In contrast to prior studies, this chapter selects as its unit of analysis the student-faculty interaction and explores its importance to the clarification of intended learning outcomes. The chapter briefly explores, through a set of possible questions one might raise, the features of a quality relationship between student and professor. The questions pave the way for two case studies that are used to permit a closer inspection of the interactive dynamic that develops in an individualized instructional relationship. Although the cases presented were not originally developed for the single purpose of studying student-faculty relationships and are not, therefore, hard evidence in support of our view about the faculty-student interaction, they do provoke questions that help further our understanding of how the learning/teaching process in this instructional mode works and also help sharpen considerations for future research. The intent of the questions posed and the case studies presented is to provoke the reader's imagination regarding the impact of an effective interpersonal dynamic on the process of clarifying learning outcomes.

This chapter concludes with the statement of a general hypothesis for future research that draws on suggestions stimulated in work done by Claxton and Ralston (1978), Fry and Kolb (1979), Messick and others (1976), and Witkin (1976). It is suggested that a match in interaction styles between student and faculty facilitates clarification of intended learning outcomes.

The Individualized Learning Process

Although little systematic research is available, our experience in observation and practice leads us to believe that the quality of the one-to-one relationship between the student and professor in individualized education is critical to effective learning. If this relationship is sensitive, strong, and challenging, then students progress intellectually because they can rely on the professor for constructive guidance and evaluation of work completed. If, on the other hand, a sour relationship develops, the results often are confusion, disappointment, and in some cases attrition. The student, while offering a variety of reasons, just drops out of the program.

Thus, it is important to know more about what seem to be the critical ingredients for the development and functioning of sensitive, strong, challenging, one-to-one (dyadic) student-professor relationships. In the following paragraphs we discuss the dynamic of this relationship, so that its role in clarifying and achieving learning outcomes can be better understood.

The first two questions concern expectations and rewards. We might phrase the first question as follows: What are the expectations held by student and professor for one another? This general question can be broken down into a number of subquestions such as: Who is responsible for identifying study topics and activities? Who will determine what components are included in the study program? How will the student's background be used in the program? Who will decide how much study is appropriate to a particular amount of credit? How will the study be evaluated? By whom?

The question about rewards might be phrased like this: Is each of the participants receiving benefits from the interaction that are personally satisfying? This general question can be subdivided according to the concerns of the student: Is the professor dealing with me as an individual? Does he or she acknowledge my background as a contribution to contracts (studies) and program components? Does the professor provide me with useful guidance when I need it? Is the work I am undertaking really important to my long-range goals?

Subquestions relative to rewards for faculty can also be posed: Is the student showing a genuine appreciation for scholarly learning? Is the student making progress in a timely and developmental way, responding to the intellectual challenges offered? Is the student willing to participate in the design of study programs, making use of opportunities and resources around him or her? Is the student willing to become a truly independent learner?

A few more words about expectations. We believe that the establishment of intended learning outcomes is facilitated when the relationship between student and faculty is supportive, focused on the student's goals, and achieves a fairly high degree of clarity relative to responsibilities. The faculty side of the relationship holds rather specific instructional and/or counseling responsibilities. When the program features shift these functions toward a different distribution from that operating in traditional classroom approaches, it is important that both faculty and student work out through discussion what the differences are and who is responsible for what parts of the learning process.

In some programs, for example, the faculty is expected to make only a limited amount of time available to the student for instruction, while the student is expected to work through learning activities independently, bringing only significant problems to conferences. The student is expected to respond to the intellectual challenges offered by the faculty, exploring widely and expanding intellectual curiosity. The faculty is expected to identify learning activities that make use of the student's previously developed background, and the student is expected to take an active part in searching for appropriate activities that are consistent with his or her program goals. The faculty is expected to provide critique in a timely and supportive manner on both the learning process and the student's products (papers, logs, activity reports, and so forth), while the student is expected to seek evaluative commentary.

In addition to expectations and rewards already discussed in regard to the student-professor relationship, some additional questions that probe the workings of the dyadic relationship are not typically asked in education. Although we have a considerable amount of information on the more obvious functioning of student-professor relationships, as will be demonstrated in the case studies to follow, there is little—if any—systematic data about the more subtle facets of the two-person dyad as it operates in educational settings. We do not know, for example, if the student truly trusts the professor or, conversely, if the professor trusts the student. How can we evaluate whether these two partners in the learning relationship respect one another or can be honest with each other?

Such questions attempt to probe the subtle but actual features of a sound working student-professor relationship. For example, it is important that the student feel it is permissible to express his or her own ideas or ideas not fully developed without being trampled on by the professor. Call it trust, respect, or tolerance: Students show evidence of considerable concern over how their thoughts and ideas will be received by the professor. This feeling is reinforced by traditional expectations that imply that the student is not knowledgeable and the professor is the expert. Students are often wary of expressing ideas that are contrary to those of faculty. Yet a productive learning relationship requires that this type of freedom be a feature of the operating environment.

When we think about honesty as a desirable quality of a two-person relationship, we are faced with an intriguing and tricky problem. It is intriguing because one seldom knows whether honesty will help or hinder the relationship. It is tricky because people play games to avoid being honest not only with others but with themselves. Students and professors would most likely prefer to be honest but often lack the certainty to know how such responses will be taken by the other party. Potential consequences—on both sides—raise cautions. For example, it may be educationally appropriate for the professor to say to the student: "Your paper is terrible; you must do better." Likewise the student might want to reply: "I don't really care what you want out of my paper. I only care what I will learn that will be useful to me." The nature of the dynamic operating in the relationship, as well as other variables we will not touch on here, influences the level of honesty that develops.

Another dimension of two-person relationships that is controversial as a component in educational relationships is friendship. Friendship can refer to the degree to which a relationship contains personal dimensions that address the total person and details of his or her life pattern. Friendship also includes liking the other person—that is, the extent to which one is interested in what the other believes, does, and thinks on a variety of issues. In student-professor relationships, a sensitive supportive relationship can take on nuances that imply personal concern on the part of the professor for the student. Typically, mentor-student relationships involve the mentor's becoming familiar with the types of problems in the student's life, particularly those that consume time and energy that might be devoted to study. Whereas it may be important to provide support and encouragement to students when things in their personal lives are not going well (as in the sickness of a spouse), this knowledge can force a conflict if students expect that such distractions from their study time relieve them of the responsibility of completing portions of the learning activities assigned. A close friendship may result in the professor's feeling compromised in carrying out the evaluation of learning in a fair and impartial manner. Similarly, the student who feels that the faculty person is a real friend may expect an overly positive response to papers and products developed during the learning process. The professor's supportive yet critical and honest evaluation may provoke a reaction on the part of the student that the professor is being disloyal.

These dimensions of a one-to-one learning relationship—rewards, trust, tolerance, honesty, and friendship—appear to contribute to good learning outcomes. Yet attention to these qualities as variables influencing learning outcomes is minimal, even nonexistent, in the literature of individualized education. Raising these issues as part of a larger concern for clarifying learning outcomes opens a fascinating new direction and stimulates thinking that is important if we are to understand the workings of individualized learning as a distinctive educational mode.

Individualized Learning Examples

In order to illustrate some of the qualities just discussed, we now present two case studies. These accounts are drawn from a larger data set collected and reported at Empire State College. (These case materials are adapted from two sources: Palola and Bradley, 1973 and Office of Research and Evaluation, 1977.) In the Empire State program, faculty serve in an instructional and counseling role as mentor, working on a one-to-one basis with students. Operating in a statewide dispersed organizational model, the college attracts students from a wide range of backgrounds and community settings. In addition to direct instruction, the mentor assists the student with several encompassing program responsibilities, including the development of a degree plan, identification of learning derived from formal and informal sources contributing to completion of that plan, assessment of prior learning from life and work experience and informal study, and the development of learning contracts.

For most students, experiential learning acquired before entering the program provides a rich base from which academic components are developed through contract learning. Learning outcomes are developed as a result of study and activities designed to contribute to the student's personal, academic, and career goals. One or more study themes are joined together in a learning contract that is guided by the primary mentor, other faculty within the college, or makes use of learning resources and opportunities found in the community where the student lives. The learning contract sets forth the goals and objectives of the study, outlines the activities that will lead to the achievement of stated objectives, and states criteria used in evaluation of the learning.

The reader is urged to keep the questions posed in the previous section in mind when examining the case study material.

Case Study 1: Sally

Sally is thirty-six years old, married, the mother of two children, has a nursing diploma, and presently works as the inservice supervisor at City Hospital in New York. She comes from a family of moderate means and has spent her entire life on the East coast. Her political views are basically liberal, and she sees Empire State College (ESC) and other forms of alternative education as the truly meaningful way to educate people in a world that is too rapidly becoming dehumanized, and insensitive.

Sally first heard about ESC through her director of nursing at City Hospital. The director was exposed to the college and its unique alternatives at a professional conference and thought it would suit Sally's goal—obtaining a bachelor's degree—while she continued working at the hospital. Credit for prior college work and life experiences was attractive to Sally, since she saw a quick bachelor's degree as a stepping stone to graduate school and a master's degree in community health education.

Sally enrolled at ESC and attended a student orientation workshop held by the Manhattan Learning Center. A faculty member, who subsequently became Sally's mentor, answered her questions about the college: Will I work with one or several mentors? Will I have a study program that really fits my interests and needs? How will my prior college credits and work experience be evaluated?

Sally spent many hours and weeks prior to developing her first contract, writing an eighty-page intellectual autobiography and several short papers on various ideas and experiences important to her. Following the challenge of her mentor, she thought that this would help her see more clearly where she was aiming professionally, how far her knowledge and wisdom about nursing had progressed, and where ESC could logically fit into her life. Sally described the value of these stocktaking opportunities in the following way:

> This was really a chance of a lifetime for me. Never before had I sat down with paper and pencil in hand and tried to realistically and honestly describe who I am, where I've been, *what I've learned,* where I'm going with my career and life, and hardest of all, to admit my weaknesses, both in terms of my knowledge and personal shortcomings. . . . So it really was a significant task for me, probably the most important single opportunity this college encouraged me to do (Palola and Bradley, 1973, p. 28).

Sally's study plan at ESC involved work in three primary areas—hospital management and administration, small group theory and research, and explorations in psychoanalytic theory. She brought to her program prior college credits, College Level Examination Program (CLEP) credit, and eight years of work experience in health care. For the learning she had developed in holding positions of progressively more and more responsibility, Sally was granted ninety-six credits of advanced standing at ESC. The faculty assessed her as follows: "She demonstrates intellectual and interpersonal competence, with considerable scientific knowledge, sufficient achievement in liberal arts as demonstrated by high scores in CLEP General Examinations, the ability to do research, absorb knowledge and conceptualize. The Committee approves her planned program of study" (p. 28).

Two twelve-credit contracts were developed and completed by Sally. The specific purposes of the first contract were stated in the following way:

> As a nurse supervisor, Sally conducts group study sessions for nurses, patients, and members of the community, provides orientation training, on-the-job or skill training for nurses, and is responsible for staff development, continuing education, and clinical supervision.
>
> She now seeks to study management and group dynamics and to find new and broader concepts which will help her understand, interpret, and add theoretical perspectives to her work.
>
> In this study plan, she will read in management theory and group dynamics—both in terms of broad theory and in application

> to the hospital environment. She will trace significant concepts as they apply to her supervisory functions, and activities and as they apply to her larger interest in community health planning [p. 28].

The bibliography of readings was long but interesting to Sally and included various works by Argyris, Dubin, Likert, Bion, Homans, and Maslow. Sally kept a log of her work experiences, working from certain key theories and tracing the development of her observations as guided by these constructs, building a set of specific information, then applying that learning to hospital work problems. Through biweekly conferences, Sally and her mentor discussed the readings, log, and papers. Her work was evaluated by her hospital supervisor in terms of contributions to managerial and group work and by her mentor, who assessed her academic learning as demonstrated in conference and papers. Sally wrote two major papers, one on the theory of management, and the other on the theory of group dynamics as they apply to community health.

The mentor's written statements about Sally's work shows the usefulness and significance of contract learning to her intellectual growth and development:

> Sally has done outstanding work on a difficult study plan and demonstrated the value of independent study for a student who is intelligent, motivated, hardworking, disciplined, and well-organized. In her readings, she has insightfully and brilliantly extracted the essential concepts and finer nuances, then systematically applied them to her own work situation, to an expanded understanding of herself and others, and to a sensitive grasp of the implications in the wider culture.
>
> Specifically, she has read diligently in group dynamics, administrative theory, and hospital administration. Her supervisor at work confirmed that Sally had developed a sound set of knowledge as evidenced by her creative contributions. Her logs report an enthusiastic and well-developed learning progress, both theoretical and applied. Her discussions with the mentor reflect the ability to sort out ideas rationally, discard some, and integrate others into her own thought processes. Her written papers were brilliant applications of theory applied to her working interests.
>
> Overall the mentor felt Sally was an excellent student, working on the level of first-rate graduate students [Palola and Bradley, 1973, p. 29].

In a second and final contract on psychoanalytic theory, Sally was exposed to the thoughts, ideas, and wisdom of such authors as Monroe, Freud, Erikson, Sullivan, and Maslow. She also looked at various social applications of psychoanalytic theory in works by Blitsen, Spiegel, Leighton, and Lynd. A third focus, thanatology, or the study of death, was pursued through works by Kubler-Ross, Kutscher, Schoenberg, and others. Sally continued to develop a log on insights gained from her work and readings. This technique allowed a considerable amount of self-assessment.

Sally's outstanding work and exceptional development during the second contract were described in the following terms by her mentor: "Sally demonstrates an unusual sophistication in handling ideas, difficult concepts, and integration of theory with practice. Her ability to capture the essence of an idea as well as the essence of an interpersonal relationship enables her to exercise her unusual intelligence in learning experiences" (Palola and Bradley, 1973, p. 30).

One of the factors contributing to Sally's success at ESC was her relationship with her mentor. The effectiveness of the student-mentor relationship at ESC appears to involve the awareness of mentors of three key characteristics of students: intellectual capability, desire and ability for independent work, and interest in a variety of academic subjects. The mentor's skill in working with these characteristics is an important contribution to the quality of the student's learning outcomes. Sally repeatedly commented on the importance of her connecting in significant social and intellectual ways with her mentor.

During her postgraduation interview, Sally was asked to describe the most significant learning outcomes, in both cognitive and affective terms, of her ESC educational activities. She listed very marked increases in interpersonal competence, awareness of self and others, self-understanding, self-consistency, greatly expanded factual knowledge, and increased capability in comprehension, analysis, evaluation, and application. She gave concrete examples to illustrate these various gains. Her reported accomplishments are directly on target with ESC's student goals and objectives.

After receiving her bachelor's degree, Sally was asked to teach basic courses in nursing at City College of New York. She said, "It is amazing when you think of it. I'm the first person without a master's degree to teach nursing courses" (Palola and Bradley, 1973, p. 30). She subsequently enrolled as a graduate student at Hunter College.

Case Study 2: Sara

Sara is forty-nine years old, married, and the mother of five children. Sara was raised in the Bedford Stuyvesant area of the New York metropolitan area but is presently living on the East side of New York. Her mother was a college graduate, employed by the federal government, and her father, also a college graduate, served as a City Councilman and later as State Assemblyman for the district.

Sara attended a public high school and graduated in the top half of her class. She trained as a medical assistant at the Mandl School of Medical Technology. In addition, she earned nine semester hours in night courses at Columbia University School of Pharmacy. In 1948, Sara had enrolled at the University of Chicago but withdrew after two years to marry and raise a family.

In the late 1950s separation from her husband forced Sara to work at two jobs in order to support her children. For ten years she worked in civil service positions, for the Internal Revenue Service and the U.S. Army, where she received training as a keypunch operator and supervisor. From 1960 to 1971, Sara was employed at Columbia University's School of Public Health, where she was involved in research activities in the fields of psychology, sociology, and public health. She worked with people who had a master's or Ph.D. degree. Her own mobility and recognition as a professional was hindered by lack of a bachelor's credential. In 1971, Sara left Columbia to accept a position as administrative assistant to the executive director of a secondary school that serves as a therapeutic community and rehabilitation center for adolescent (ages thirteen to nineteen) drug and alcohol abusers. She performs not only administrative functions but is also involved in various aspects of the rehabilitation of clients. An article in a community newspaper about Empire State College at Bedford Stuyvesant induced her to investigate the program and subsequently enroll at the Bedford Stuyvesant Unit. The ability to receive credit for prior learning experiences and the independence in study mode allowed by the college were very influential in her decision to enroll.

Sara's prime objective at ESC was to get a BA degree in community and human services, but, in addition, she hoped to obtain specific job-related skills, develop a new career, and be able to meet the academic requirements necessary to enter graduate school.

In the general essay of her portfolio, Sara documented learnings from prior academic work, work experiences, and participation in numerous civic organizations. However, advanced standing was requested mainly for transcript credit, for which she received eighty-six credits. In addition, eight credits of advanced standing were requested and granted for data processing knowledge gained in working at Columbia University. The remaining twenty-six credits needed for her degree were earned with learning contracts in the following: Urban Health Problems and Teen-Age Addicts Research Project, twelve credits; residency on criminal justice and proposal writings, four credits; women's liberation movement, 10 credits.

For her first contract, Sara participated in a seminar, Health Problems of the Urban Community, in order to increase her knowledge of the medical and psychosocial attributes of health problems. The two-month seminar was held once a week at the Metropolitan Center and covered problems of infants and children and addiction, behavior-modification drugs and social policy on drugs. Sara submitted a final paper, "Drug Addiction: Treatment and Problems," that the seminar leader considered "one of the finest submitted. It was carefully organized, well documented and full of information. The student discussed at length present drug programs, giving her own opinions and estimates of the programs as well as those of other experts. I found the paper to be a valuable addition to my knowledge of drug abuse and its treatment" (Office of Research and Evaluation, Empire State College, 1977, p. 41).

The second portion of the contract involved a follow-up study of adolescents who withdrew from the rehabilitation school against the advice of the counselors. Sara designed the project, implemented it, computerized the data, and submitted a final report of the findings. Her bibliography included the basic research methods text by Seltiz and selected issues of *Mental Health and Hygiene, Journal of Personnel,* and *Guidance and Rehabilitation Counseling*. She has reviewed and assessed follow-up studies on the evaluation of Phoenix House and the Lower East Side Service School. The mentor evaluated Sara on her ability to set up an appropriate research design and execute it: "Her attitude in proceeding through the necessary steps in a research design—that is, moving from the identification of a problem through the implications of her study was that of a skilled researcher. Her final product was well organized, well written, highly documented, and generally an excellent piece of research (Office of Research and Evaluation, Empire State College, 1977, p. 42).

The learning activities of Sara's second contract were chosen to broaden her understanding of the criminal justice system. She participated in a week-long residency conducted by the New York City Department of Correction, where the following topics were addressed:

- The view from inside: what takes place in prisons, behavior modification, isolationism, strategies used by prisoners to exist from day to day
- The view from outside: system planning, obstacles to public scrutiny of the prisons, after-care programs.
- Alternatives: what can be done about prisons, how can effective action be organized.

Participants in the residency were also requested to submit a final project that would constitute an extensive study of a significant aspect of the criminal justice system. Sara's project was entitled "A Proposal for Pretrial Information for Juvenile Delinquents." Her readings for the residency included several articles from correction magazines and works by Mitford, Jackson, Dostoyevski, Kafka, and Alcabes.

Sara's proposal was developed as a result of what she learned from the residency and her experiences with adolescents. She proposed a prevention program that would reach children under the age of thirteen who have a history of antisocial behavior. Sara described her learning experiences:

"I had never written a proposal before—assessing the target area, determining the needs, writing a job description, writing the prospectus stating why I felt this type of organization was needed. It was truly a significant learning experience" (Office of Research and Evaluation, Empire State College, 1977, p. 43).

Sara later tried to obtain funding from various organizations and received some positive reactions, especially from the Boy Scouts of America. However, acceptance of the proposal was dependent upon Sara's changing some of the aspects of the program, and lack of time because of job and school commitments necessitated postponement of her efforts.

The residency leader evaluated her work as follows: "Preparation by the student was more than adequate for positive participation in all phases of the residency. Class participation in discussion and personal input was of the highest caliber. Clarity, scope, and comprehension of the elements of the juvenile criminal justice chosen for analysis are readily discerned" (Office of Research and Evaluation, Empire State College, 1977, p. 43).

Analysis of the Case Studies

Several questions were presented earlier in order to stimulate thinking and guide the analysis of the case study material. While others are possible, three observations seem most relevant to the question of clarifying learning outcomes. The first observation is that contract learning is an effective mechanism for promoting sound learning outcomes and clarifying student-professor relationships. Students see contracts as a means by which study can be directed in a flexible yet intellectually challenging way. Learning modes can be mixed to accomplish various goals, some theoretical, others experiential and applied. Contracts are often written with both student and mentor contributing to the design of objectives, selection of learning activities, and evaluation criteria. These joint activities involving the student serve to demonstrate how one moves from intended outcomes—articulated in statements of study objectives—to actual outcomes. The student is a participant in this design process and the one responsible for carrying out the implementation of the study.

In the case study of Sally, we can see the importance of contracts and the portfolio development process to clarifying intended outcomes. She explains that these activities required her for the first time in her life to sit down and assess her past experience and project what she had learned toward the development of future plans. Sara also identifies several personal, developmental outcomes: interpersonal competence, awareness of self and others, self-consistency, and how to organize for formal presentation.

A second observation is that important differences exist in the way faculty approach their role as individualized educators. In a tutorial approach, faculty are responsible for direct instruction; they serve as teacher. The faculty person—often designated as mentor—guides the learning process, serving as tutor and educational resource person. In a facilitative approach, less time is devoted to direct instruction; rather, extrainstitutional resources are identified by the faculty to support and enrich the student's learning experience. Both approaches usually require face-to-face contact at least in the planning and evaluation stages. In the tutorial role, faculty draw on disciplinary expertise and can guide and mold outcomes through expectations set for products (for example, papers, projects, journals, and so forth). In this role, faculty can contribute to both cognitive and affective student growth. Sally's mentor seems to illustrate this approach with his strong guiding and shaping behavior. In the facilitative role, faculty identify other resource people to monitor and guide student learning activities. Because of the diminished role in the student's educational development, faculty often encourage the student to take on what might be considered faculty responsibilities (such as identifying bibliography, setting evaluation modes and criteria, and identifying appropriate learning activities). This approach is illustrated by Sara's mentor, who guides her in the use of various community resources. In both approaches, faculty are responsible for articulating intended outcomes and evaluating actual ones. In the role of facilitator, faculty responsibility is often to draw together and document learning as described from a resource person or field-based sponsor.

A third observation is that students need the supportive encouragement of mentors to develop solid learning outcomes. The case studies illustrate that supportive approaches facilitate student success. A striking reality for mentors is that many students have full agendas, including family, work, and community commitments. Mentors often must help adult students sort out priorities, identify difficulties encountered in the study process, find study resources, and think and rethink conceptual problems encountered in writing papers.

As the case study material vividly illustrates, the outcomes accruing to the student are developmentally important. The individualized process allows students to assess their strengths and weaknesses. The self-assessment activities necessary to identify, articulate, and document learning for a degree program serve to indicate where academic and skill development is best focused. This information frequently allows faculty to suggest learning activities that fill in the gaps. In actuality, the degree program planning activity serves as a clarification process that allows faculty to provide instruction on many aspects of learning that are important to developmental goals for adults.

The case studies are supplemented by data gathered at Empire State College describing a larger sample of students completing the program. Drawing one example from those findings will illustrate the influence of the student-mentor relationship in more detail. The interactive dynamic emerges as an important contributor to learning outcomes (Table 1). From these data, one can infer that, although the student's agenda is of central importance, intellectual stimulation and challenge are part of the faculty contribution to the dynamic. Inherent to a satisfying interaction in the learning situation is subtle encouragement to the student to become more and more independent as a learner. In fact, we have observed that when the relationship truly is successful, the student's confidence in his or her own ability to perform at high levels is clearly evident.

A Proposed Interaction Hypothesis

There is little new or shocking about the observation that how well two people get along will markedly affect what they can jointly accomplish. Some argue that calm and cooperative relationships lead to the most effective results. Others say that a kind of dynamic tension in relationships

Table 1. Student Relationships with Mentor During the Contract-Learning Process

Characteristics	*Never* # (%)	*Occasionally* # (%)	*Frequently* # (%)	*Almost always* # (%)	*Undecided* # (%)	*NA* #
My mentor challenged me to work at a level higher than I expected	19 (7)	50 (18)	85 (31)	112 (40)	13 (5)	10
My mentor often made me think through difficult questions rather than provide answers	13 (5)	37 (13)	102 (36)	120 (43)	10 (4)	7
My mentor clearly took into account my personal desires in planning the degree program	5 (2)	19 (7)	62 (22)	189 (67)	9 (3)	5
My mentor eased my anxieties when I worried about contract work	18 (7)	56 (21)	70 (26)	116 (43)	11 (4)	18
The relationship with my mentor was educationally effective	5 (2)	20 (7)	41 (15)	213 (76)	2 (1)	8
The relationship with my mentor was personally satisfying	10 (4)	23 (8)	49 (17)	197 (70)	3 (1)	7
My mentor let me have "lots of rope" to pursue my goals	3 (1)	28 (10)	74 (27)	163 (58)	11 (4)	10

has the greatest likelihood of creating important achievements. Few would agree that open conflict or hostility is conducive to good results. But the surprising thing about each of these generalizations—common as they may appear—is that they do not predict behavior in learning settings with much accuracy. Why? The answer, if there is one, seems to be related to our tendency to oversimplify two-person relationships and the number and importance of different variables and influences that are at work in these relationships. What this leads us to suggest is that we probably have not figured out student-professor relationships, and much more study is needed.

We propose that the amount of learning the student accomplishes in an individualized form of education depends on the quality of the relationship between the student and his or her mentor. Beyond this more or less obvious point, we have tried to suggest in this chapter what some of the important dimensions of this relationship might be: clear expectations for student and professor, rewards suited to each participant's needs, mutual trust and respect, tolerance for each other's foibles and ideas, and some degree of friendship. We can all cite cases from personal experience that would fit nicely into this construct. But we think more is needed. And we think that, before we can add to our substantive knowledge, a restructured research design and a well-executed approach systematically and scientifically examining two-person relationships in educational settings is needed. There is some research (Fry and Kolb, 1979; Kagan and Wallach, 1965; Rosenthal and Jacobson, 1968; Witkin, 1969, 1976) that already provides direction. No one, to our knowledge, has focused specifically on the quality of the relationship between professor and student, taking this relationship as the unit of analysis and examining what makes it work. We encourage attention to how the nature of the relationship adds to or subtracts from student learning and in what ways a quality relationship contributes to students' progress.

References

Berte, N. (Ed.). *Individualizing Education Through Contract Learning*. Tuscaloosa: University of Alabama, 1976.

Bradley, A. P., Jr. "Faculty Roles in Contract Learning." In D. Vermilye (Ed.), *Current Issues in Higher Education: Learner-Centered Reform*. San Francisco: Jossey-Bass, 1975.

Bradley, A. P., Jr. *The New Professional: A Report on Faculty in Individualized Education*. Saratoga Springs, N.Y.: Empire State College, Office of Research and Evaluation, 1978.

Clark, F. T. *New Academic Programs/New Professional Roles: A Description of Individualized Education and Faculty Development at Eight Institutions*. Saratoga Springs, N.Y.: Empire State College, Center for Individualized Education, 1975.

Claxton, C., and Ralston, Y. *Learning Styles: Their Impact on Teaching and Administration.* American Association for Higher Education-ERIC, Higher Education Research Report No. 10. Washington, D.C.: American Association for Higher Education, 1978.

Eldred, M. D., and Marienau, C. *Adult Baccalaureate Programs.* American Association for Higher Education-ERIC, Higher Education Research Report No. 9. Washington, D.C.: American Association for Higher Education, 1979.

Fry, R., and Kolb, D. "Experiential Learning Theory and Learning in Liberal Arts Education." In S. E. Brooks and J. A. Althof (Eds.), *New Directions for Experiential Learning: Enriching the Liberal Arts Through Experiential Learning,* no. 6. San Francisco: Jossey-Bass, 1979.

Fund for the Improvement of Postsecondary Education. *Designing for Development: Four Programs for Adult Undergraduates.* Washington, D.C.: Fund for the Improvement of Postsecondary Education, no date.

Hall, J., and Palola, E. "Curricula for Adult Learners." *Canadian Journal of University Continuing Education,* 1981, *7* (2), 36–40.

Henderson, H., and Hyre, S. "Contract Learning." In S. E. Brooks and J. Althof, *New Directions for Experiential Learning: Enriching the Liberal Arts through Experiential Learning,* no. 6. San Francisco: Jossey-Bass, 1979.

Johnson, J. N. *University of Minnesota Faculty Participation in the University Without Walls.* Monograph 1. Yellow Springs, Ohio: Union Press, 1975.

Kagan, N., and Wallach, M. A. *Risk Taking.* New York: Holt, Rinehart and Winston, 1965.

Lehmann, T. "Educational Outcomes from Contract Learning at Empire State College." Paper presented at American Association of Higher Education, National Conference on Higher Education, March 24, 1975.

Lehmann, T. "Do Men and Women in Transition Have Different Education Needs?" Paper presented at Second National Conference on the Adult Life Cycle, Overland Park, Kansas, November 23-25, 1980.

Medsker, L., Edelstein, S., Kraplin, H., Ruyle, J., and Shea, J. *Extending Opportunities for a College Degree: Practices, Problems, and Potentials.* Berkeley: Center for Research and Development in Higher Education, University of California, 1975.

Messick, S., and Associates. *Individuality in Learning: Implications of Cognitive Styles and Creativity for Human Development.* San Francisco: Jossey-Bass, 1976.

Office of Research and Evaluation, Empire State College. "Bedford Stuyvesant Unit Evaluation." Saratoga Springs, N.Y.: Office of Research and Evaluation, Empire State College, 1977.

Palola, E., and Bradley, P. "Ten Out of Thirty: Studies of First Graduates of Empire State College." Saratoga Springs, N.Y.: Office of Research and Evaluation, Empire State College, 1973.

Peterson, R., and Associates. *Lifelong Learning in America: An Overview of Current Practices, Available Resources, and Future Prospects.* San Francisco: Jossey-Bass, 1979.

Rosenthal, R., and Jacobson, L. *Pygmalion in the Classroom.* New York: Holt, Rinehart and Winston, 1968.

Vermilye, D. (Ed.). *Current Issues in Higher Education: Individualizing the System.* San Francisco: Jossey-Bass, 1976.

Wald, R. "Confronting the Learning Contract." *Alternative Higher Education,* 1978, *2* (3), 223–231.

Weathersby, R., and Tarule, J. *Adult Development: Implications for Higher Education.* Report No. 4. Washington, D.C.: American Association for Higher Education, 1980.

Witkin, H. A. "Social Influences in the Development of Cognitive Style." In D. Goslin (Ed.), *Handbook of Socialization Theory and Research.* Chicago: Rand McNally, 1969.

Witkin, H. A. "Cognitive Style in Academic Performance and in Teacher-Student Relations." In S. Messick and Associates (Eds.), *Individuality in Learning: Implications of Cognitive Styles and Creativity for Human Development.* San Francisco: Jossey-Bass, 1976.

Ernest G. Palola has been conducting research on the social organization of higher education for twenty years, and has published on individualized education, learning outcomes, educational and organizational evaluation, stress management, and national planning. He organized the Office of Research and Evaluation at Empire State College, an institution recognized for innovative approaches to learning services for adults. Currently he is organizing a research institute that will conduct studies on several themes important to professional-client relationships in adult development.

Marlene J. Evans has served for seven years as mentor/coordinator at Empire State College in the Center for Statewide Programs. While serving for two years as acting associate dean, she intensified her interest in the relationship between faculty and student and the influence of different mentoring styles on adult learning. She is currently engaged in research that supplements earlier work done on perceptual and attitudinal responses to educational information.

The major ideas developed in the sourcebook provide insights for faculty and administrators considering the clarification of educational outcomes. The experiences of the institutions studied suggest a set of flexibly structured guidelines for strategies to implement the process. The questions raised prompt future actions and research ideas.

Rethinking and Implementing Outcome Clarification

Marlene J. Evans
Georgine Loacker
Ernest G. Palola

While the central theme of this sourcebook is clarifying learning outcomes, the viewpoints of the authors are not singular in focus or intent. Not only do they represent a variety of interpretations of what outcomes mean but they also show different perspectives on where to begin and what hinders or encourages the clarifying process. They mirror the kind of rich diversity one expects when a group of professionals with a wide range of backgrounds comment on a given topic. In this chapter, we will draw out some common themes and individual insights that combine to suggest the state of the art. We pose two questions as organizing frameworks: What have we learned about the process of clarifying learning outcomes? What new directions arise from thinking and rethinking that process?

A number of points appear to stand out in our review and synthesis of the sourcebook's chapters. First is the fact that faculty are in danger of losing their status as professionals who set and interpret their own content, process, and standards. Society is questioning the right of educators to make curricular decisions unilaterally. A critical issue for faculty over the next decade is how to meet this challenge nondefensively by a willingness to heed and evaluate pragmatic concerns, remaining true to the idealism of higher education, while simultaneously providing students with the necessary practical content to meet economic and job market pressures.

Another point to be considered is that, as part of reestablishing their professionalism, faculty need to take responsibility for clarifying learning outcomes—both expected and actual. Though students can benefit by clarifying their individual learning goals, faculty are primarily responsible for the quality of student learning. Therefore faculty need to clarify expected outcomes in relation to the disciplinary content they have been trained to profess, while making appropriate linkages to the students' professional requirements and personal goals. In individualized education, faculty and student may find that negotiations are appropriate so that reasonable compromises between faculty professional responsibilities and student pragmatic concerns can be made.

In individualized education programs, the quality of interaction between student and professor has important implications for student learning and outcomes. The range of outcomes for students seems to be affected by the nature and quality of the relationship between student and professor. The nature and quality of the relationship include such factors as clarity of expectations and the roles and responsibilities of both student and professor. Other important contributing factors, though not yet systematically tested, include trust, respect, tolerance, and friendship.

Once an institution has made the commitment to clarify expected outcomes, a new dynamism is often sparked in the learning process. Examination of the activity at institutions where such commitment among the faculty has occurred shows that it tends to establish and increase collaboration between departments. When a discipline underscores the importance of clarifying outcomes so that development of ability is related to intellectual understanding, the necessity to bridge disciplines arises.

Faculty need an environment that supports the teaching role and all its implications. Academic procedure, as well as the daily perspectives of administrators, must be dedicated to the achievement of student learning outcomes. This is best accomplished by consistent institutional support of faculty in their regular work with students. Once the outcome clarifying process begins, it is of basic importance to be aware of the social context of the learning and teaching environment, and to recognize the norms operating for both student and faculty.

In addition, when faculty clarify their personal philosophies, they contribute significantly to the clarifying of student outcomes. The philosophical orientation of individual faculty can shape the kinds of content and quality of expectations held for student learning. Philosophical positions influence the purposes and intent of a teaching approach.

An important challenge for faculty is the integration of affective with cognitive components in student learning outcomes. Traditionally, faculty tend to focus mainly, if not exclusively, on the cognitive realm—that is to say, the ideas, facts, and interpretations of knowledge in their disciplines. However, student learning always includes affective components, at least in the form of attitudes about the quality of one's written work or the quality of relationship among members in a group learning experience. Faculty need to give attention to these components if effective learning outcomes are to be developed.

As faculty clarify the learning outcomes of the institution, a process develops. Neither a rigid, preestablished set of outcomes nor a mechanistic or atomistic statement of specific behaviors or tasks should result. The process should continue to change in response to societal and individual student needs, as well as faculty viewpoints.

Is There a Model?

From the varied perspectives in this sourcebook, is it possible to identify a model approach to clarifying outcomes? It does not seem so, since opening questions vary: How can we improve our educational process? How can we find out if we are doing what we promise? What is unique about our graduates? How can we assure graduating students that they have the skills their employers want? Processes already in operation at varied institutions suggest that one might select a number of factors that affect and are, in turn, affected by clarifying outcomes:

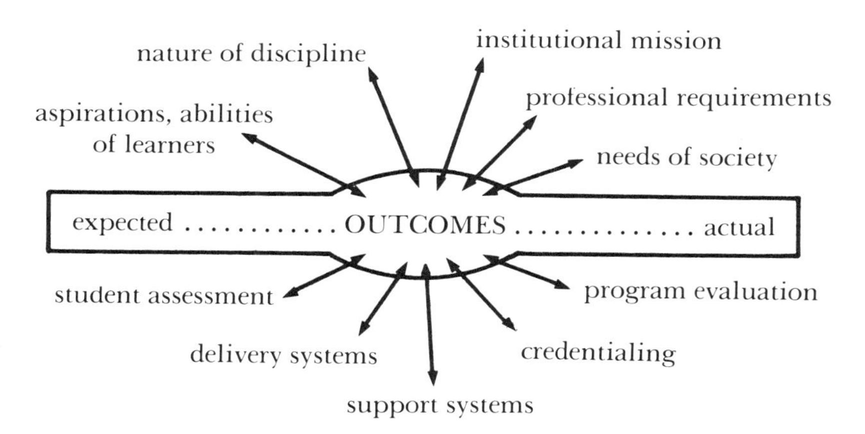

No matter what approach we use in clarifying expected outcomes, we can move from degree or program to individual course or in the opposite direction. Almost any of the elements (initiation points) can serve as places to enter the system. Some elements like *needs of society* or *student aspirations and abilities* require considerably more research. If faculty, individually or in groups, choose to clarify expected outcomes by making inferences from generalized experience, they will come up with some kind of hypothetical description of the person who has learned—for example, in their course, in their institution, for a given profession. The description of such a learner can take multiple forms, depending on the style of the person(s) clarifying outcomes. It can be generated in brainstorming sessions or by some systematic method using consensus, such as the Delphi technique, which creates a kind of statistical consensus by polling individual preferences. It can be a general, even idealized, statement that can gradually be rewritten more concretely to become a list of expected functional outcomes.

If, on the other hand, faculty choose to use a method of inferring actual outcomes from existing data in order to examine them critically, they can also begin with almost any element in either sector of the diagram. An analysis of existing courses or of present student performance, for example, might raise those questions leading to articulating expected outcomes.

For faculty working in individualized programs to assist learners in clarifying expected outcomes, the aspirations and abilities of the student serve as the starting point. And, in fact, the interactive process between learner and mentor is, in essence, the gradual articulating of outcomes and the mapping out of their relationship to other essential elements such as assessment and credentialing and, possibly, to some selected ones, such as professional requirements.

Once we are serious about the decision to clarify outcomes and pursue the implications of this decision, we have reestablished our responsibility as professionals who serve society by serving learning. We become willing as a result of the larger process to articulate our expectations and analyze our personal approaches. Once we have recaptured those rights and their inherent obligations, clarifying outcomes itself may seem less than a gargantuan task and one well worth the winning.

Where Do We Go from Here? Future Directions

We conclude this sourcebook with a few suggestions about the future work to be done on the clarification of learning outcomes in post-secondary education. In two broad categories of suggestions we categorize our suggestions as *actions,* activities that can be undertaken in the immediate future, and *research,* areas where more information and understanding is needed.

Actions. There are a number of activities institutions can engage in, singly and collectively, based on their experience with the outcome clarification process. First, some institutions have several years of work to draw on in wrestling with the outcome clarification process. One major task for these institutions is to examine the implications of this work in various functional areas (such as curriculum redesign, use of varied learning resources, faculty workload, distribution of support staff, and so forth). Another task is to share successes and setbacks with each other.

A second set of activities would involve those institutions that show an interest in initiating the process of clarifying outcomes. These institutions need to draw on the experiences of others and seek ways to work together on problems that involve adapting the available techniques and approaches to suit local interests, talents, and needs.

A third group of activities would involve institutions whose current educational approach uses portfolio and assessment of prior learning as part of the educational process. These institutions could profit by jointly examining student statements of outcomes as a means of identifying levels of sophistication in learning.

Both traditional and nontraditional institutional faculties would benefit from participating in workshops related to clarifying outcomes. Especially needed are such topics as: (1) the meaning and significance of outcomes; (2) the general process of clarifying outcomes; (3) critique of models for clarifying outcomes; (4) designing and implementation strategies for clarification models suited to local needs, priorities, and interests; (5) analyzing learning/teaching styles in relation to implementing the process of clarifying outcomes; and (6) specifying outcomes in specific disciplines.

Research. Rather than elaborate research approaches that could be undertaken, we would like instead to suggest some reasonably clear questions that researchers might consider to provoke further study:

1. How do actual learning outcomes relate to expected outcomes?
2. What aspects of learning experiences contribute most to achieved outcomes?
3. In an individualized program, how does faculty style affect the interactive clarification of learning outcomes and the achievement of actual outcomes?
4. How should learning outcomes in professional areas relate to present professional requirements?
5. What part does content play in actually achieved outcomes?

Additional Resources

The following handbooks and articles incorporate models and/or guides for clarifying outcomes and for related processes.

Alverno College Faculty. *Assessment at Alverno College.* Milwaukee: Alverno Publications, 1979.

Alverno College Faculty. *Liberal Learning at Alverno College.* Milwaukee: Alverno Publications, 1976.

American Association of State Colleges and Universities. *The Academic Program Evaluation Project* (Marina Buhler-Miko, Director; Lin Webster, Senior Research Associate). Washington, D.C.: Resource Center for Planned Change, American Association of State Colleges and Universities, 1980.

Council for the Advancement of Experiential Learning (CAEL). *Faculty Handbook Series on Clarifying College Learning Outcomes:*

Cook, M. *Clarifying College Learning Outcomes: Developing Program Maps, Module 1.* Columbia, Md.: CAEL, 1978.

Cook, M. *Developing Learning Outcomes, Module 2.* Columbia, Md.: CAEL, 1978.

Cook, M., and Walbesser, H. *Developing Assessment Tasks, Module 3.* Columbia, Md.: CAEL, 1980.

Cook, M. *Sample Learning Maps, Module 4.* Forthcoming.

Empire State College. *1978–79 Handbook.* Saratoga Springs, N.Y.: Empire State College, 1978.

Gray, R., and Associates. *Student-Outcomes Questionnaires: An Implementation Handbook.* Boulder, Colo.: National Center for Higher Education Management Systems, 1979.

Lenning, O. *A Structure for the Outcomes of Postsecondary Education.* Boulder, Colo.: National Center for Higher Education Management Systems, 1977.

Palola, E., and Associates. *PERC (Program Effectiveness and Related Costs) Handbook.* Saratoga Springs, N.Y.: Empire State College, 1977.

Warren, J. "The Measurement of Academic Competence." Berkeley, Calif.: Educational Testing Service, 1978.

Contact people at specific institutions involved in clarifying outcomes:

Alverno College (Milwaukee, Wis. 53215): Georgine Loacker
Bowling Green University (Bowling Green, Ohio 43403): Thomas Travis
Brigham Young University (Provo, Utah 84601): Fred Rowe
Brookdale Community College (Lincroft, N.J. 07738): Rita Donahue
Bunker Hill Community College (Charlestown, Md. 02129): Elizabeth J. Noyes
Clayton Junior College (Morrow, Ga. 30260): Brad Rice
College for Human Services (New York, N.Y. 10014): President
Community College of Vermont (Montpelier, Vt. 05602): G. Richard Eisele
Delaware Community College (Media, Pa. 19063): James Donald
Eastern Oregon State (La Grande, Oreg. 97850): Jerry Young
Empire State (Saratoga Springs, N.Y. 12866): John Jacobson (Individualized Program)

Governor State College (Park Forest South, Ill. 60466): Curtis McCray
Iowa Wesleyan College (Mount Pleasant, Iowa 52641): Thomas Clayton
Kirkhof College (Allendale, Mich. 49401): Milton Ford
Mars Hill College (Mars Hill, N.C. 28754): David Knisley
Mary College (Bismarck, N. Dak. 58501): Tom Johnson
Mount Marty College (Yankton, S. Dak. 57078): Chuck Hormann
North Adams State College (North Adams, Mass. 01247): Richard Markham
Northern Virginia Community College (Annandale, Va. 22003): Arnold Oliver
Northwestern School of Music (Evanston, Ill. 60201): Jack Pernecky
Our Lady of the Lake University of San Antonio (San Antonio, Tex. 78285): Virginia Clare Duncan
Pioneer Community College (Kansas City, Mo. 64111): Dr. Queen Randall
University College of Massachusetts at Boston, Public and Community Services (Boston, Mass. 02125): Dean
University College, University of Louisville (Louisville, Ky. 40208): Mark Blum

Marlene J. Evans has served for seven years as mentor/coordinator at Empire State College in the Center for Statewide Programs. While serving for two years as acting associate dean, she intensified her interest in the relationship between faculty and student and the influence of different mentoring styles on adult learning. She is currently engaged in research that supplements earlier work done on perceptual and attitudinal responses to educational information.

Georgine Loacker is chair of the Division of Communications and of the Assessment Council at Alverno College, Milwaukee, Wisconsin. As a professor of English at Alverno, she participated in the development of its outcome-oriented education and has served as a consultant to liberal arts faculty in colleges and universities that have sought to identify and/or assess learning outcomes. She has served as a board member and regional manager for the Council for the Advancement of Experiential Learning (CAEL), as well as designer and presenter of CAEL workshops.

Ernest G. Palola has been conducting research on the social organization of higher education for twenty years, and has published on individualized education, learning outcomes, education and organizational evaluation, stress management, and national planning. He organized the Office of Research and Evaluation at Empire State College, an institution recognized for innovative approaches to learning services for adults. Currently he is organizing a research institute that will conduct studies on several themes important to professional-client relationships in adult development.

Index

N

O

P

R

S

T

U

V

W

Y

Council for the Advancement of Experiential Learning Board of Trustees (1981–1982)

Publications Available from CAEL

Assessing Occupational Competences—A CAEL Handbook, Amiel Sharon
College-Sponsored Experiential Learning—A CAEL Handbook, John Duley and Sheila Gordon
College-Sponsored Experiential Learning—A CAEL Student Guide, Hadley and Nesbitt
"Developing and Expanding Cooperative Education," *New Directions for Experiential Learning,* number 2, Pamela J. Tate and Morris T. Keeton, Editors
Efficient Evaluation of Individual Performance in Field Placement, Stephen L. Yelon and John S. Duley
Lifelong Learning: Purposes and Priorities, K. Patricia Cross

New Directions Quarterly Sourcebooks

New Directions for Experiential Learning is one of several distinct series of quarterly sourcebooks published by Jossey-Bass. The sourcebooks in each series are designed to serve both as *convenient compendiums* of the latest knowledge and practical experience on their topics and as *long-life reference tools.*

One-year, four-sourcebook subscriptions for each series cost $18 for individuals (when paid by personal check) and $30 for institutions, libraries, and agencies. Single copies of earlier sourcebooks are available at $6.95 each *prepaid* (or $7.95 each when *billed*).

A complete listing is given below of current and past sourcebooks in the *New Directions for Experiential Learning* series. The titles and editors-in-chief of the other series are also listed. To subscribe, or to receive further information, write: New Directions Subscriptions, Jossey-Bass Inc., Publishers, 433 California Street, San Francisco, California 94104.

New Directions for Experiential Learning
Pamela J. Tate, Editor-in-Chief
Morris T. Keeton, Consulting Editor

1978–1979:
1. *Learning by Experience—What, Why, How,* Morris T. Keeton, Pamela J. Tate
2. *Developing and Expanding Cooperative Education,* James W. Wilson
3. *Defining and Measuring Competence,* Paul S. Pottinger, Joan Goldsmith
4. *Transferring Experiential Credit,* S. V. Martorana, Eileen Kuhns

1979–1980:
5. *Combining Career Development with Experiential Learning,* Frank D. van Aalst
6. *Enriching the Liberal Arts Through Experiential Learning,* Stevens Brooks, James Althof
7. *Developing New Adult Clienteles by Recognizing Prior Learning,* Rexford G. Moon, Gene R. Hawes
8. *Developing Experiential Learning Programs for Professional Education,* Eugene T. Byrne, Douglas E. Wolfe

1980–1981:
9. *Defining and Assuring Quality in Experiential Learning,* Morris T. Keeton
10. *Building New Alliances: Labor Unions and Higher Education,* Hal Stack, Carroll M. Hutton
11. *Cross-Cultural Learning,* Charles B. Neff